THE SHORTER

HEAVEN AND HELL

This book is a shortened version of one written in
Latin by Emanuel Swedenborg and published in
Amsterdam in 1768. It has been compiled by Julian
Duckworth and Trevor Moffat, using the English
translation published in 1958 by the Swedenborg
Society. Readers who find this version appealing are
recommended to consult the full work or other books
presenting the ideas from it. A list is given at the end
of this volume, with addresses where they can be
obtained.

THE SHORTER

Heaven and Hell

by

Emanuel Swedenborg

Abridged by Julian Duckworth and Trevor Moffat

SEMINAR BOOKS
LONDON

THE SHORTER HEAVEN AND HELL

Published by Seminar Books
Swedenborg House, 20-21 Bloomsbury Way
London WC1A 2TH

First Edition 1993
© Copyright, this edition 1993, Seminar Books
ISBN 0 907295 20 7

Printed in Great Britain by Battle Instant Print Ltd
143 St Georges Road, Hastings, East Sussex TN34 3NF.

Designed by G. Roland Smith MCSD.

Set in 10 on 12pt Palatino by
Southern Origination Services,
76 Mount Pleasant Road, Hastings,
East Sussex TN34 3SN

British Library Cataloguing-in-Publication Data.
A catalogue record for this book is available
from the British Library.

Cover design by G. Roland Smith MCSD.

CONTENTS

CONTENTS

FOREWORD

"But no one's come back to tell us, have they?"
— So people often complain when the subject
of life after death comes up.

In these days of expert resuscitation,
thousands of people have had amazing "near
death experiences" of strangely consistent
character, which some reckon *are* instances of
such coming back. And all through history
there have been varied mystics, shamans,
visionaries, and mediums whose experiences
present similar features. But no one has
claimed longer or more detailed experiences of
the spiritual dimension than Emanuel Swedenborg, the 18th century scholar, nor analy-
sed them with more skill, insight and thor-
oughness than he did.

"Heaven and Hell" in which he gathered
systematically most of his observations on this
subject has seen many editions, has been
translated into numerous languages, and im-
pressed countless people, but it has frightened
others with its length and detail. In this
edition Julian Duckworth and Trevor Moffat,
both committed and well-read students of
Swedenborg, have selected about one sixth of
the complete work to produce a short and
readable book which still retains the essential
ideas of the original.

As well as abbreviating the text, they have omitted many Bible quotations and references which simply confirm the subject matter, though retaining those that have a direct bearing in what is being discussed. They have omitted most of Swedenborg's individual experiences of the spiritual world, while including a number that serve to clarify the subject matter. They have left out Swedenborg's paragraph numbering, but this can be found in the Appendix. They have divided his section on Heaven into two parts, to indicate a distinction between more philosophical and more descriptive topics.

Ian P. Johnson

THE AUTHOR

Emanuel Swedenborg was a man with remarkable insight and foresight.

Living from 1688 to 1772, and having absorbed most of the philosophy and scientific knowledge then available, he made significant contributions to the development of metallurgy, engineering, physics, astronomy, physiology and psychology.

As in middle age his interest turned more to philosophy and religion, he found himself in touch with inner worlds of the spirit, developed extraordinary visionary powers, perceived new depths of meaning in the Bible, and felt called to proclaim a new age of freedom and spirituality in religion. This he believed to be symbolised by the descent of the New Jerusalem from Heaven, described in the Book of Revelation.

Swedenborg's own introduction to 'Heaven and Hell'

In Matthew's gospel, in chapter 24, the Lord speaks about the 'end of the age':

"Immediately after the tribulation of those days, the sun will be darkened and the moon will not give its light; the stars will fall from heaven and the powers of the heavens will be shaken. Then the sign of the Son of Man will appear in heaven and all the tribes of the earth will mourn, and they will see the Son of Man coming on the clouds of heaven with power and great glory. And he will send his angels with a great sound of a trumpet, and they will gather together his elect from the four winds, from one end of heaven to the other."

Those who take these words to be literally true believe that these events will take place in due course. They expect the disappearance of the whole world to be replaced by a new heaven and a new earth. Yet the Word is written as it is in order to contain a deeper spiritual meaning within it, in every single phrase and detail, for the Word is written in pure correspondences, or spiritual images.

This passage from Matthew symbolically describes how the 'Church' or the degree of spiritual awareness in people can decline when they have lost their love for the Lord and their faith in him.

The majority of people are unaware of the true nature of life after death, or even that there is an afterlife. They say, "Who has ever come back and told us?" Yet these truths are contained within the Word. I have been permitted by the Lord to meet angels and spirits for many years and to talk with them, even with spirits in hell, in order to prevent further disbelief and confusion. This book is the result of this communication and it has been written so that people may know the true nature of life after death.

THE FORM OF HEAVEN

IN HEAVEN THE LORD IS GOD

It is essential first to understand the nature of God before any consideration is given to heaven and hell, because everything else depends on this fundamental point. In the whole of heaven only the Lord is worshipped as God. The angels say that they can only think of one God who is the Lord. They add that if they were to believe in three separate persons as God, they would become confused, and this itself would prevent them from entering heaven where it is impossible to say one thing and mean another. In heaven, beliefs and thoughts are known to all and are even seen on the faces of angels. It should be known, though, that those who are good but who have come to believe wrong ideas about God, can be eventually received into heaven and there be taught the truth that the Lord is God.

Those who deny that the Lord is God find themselves outside heaven if they have confirmed this belief in themselves. Such people eventually lose the ability to think clearly. The truth is simply this: that there can only be heaven where the Lord is received and where he is known to be the universal God.

Young children who die — who make up a third of heaven — are brought up in heaven to love the Lord as their heavenly Father and to know that he is the Lord of everyone.

THE LORD'S DIVINE LIFE IS WHAT MAKES HEAVEN

The angels all together are called 'heaven' because they themselves make heaven. But it is the Lord's own divine life, flowing into the angels and received by them, that makes heaven what it is. All love and understanding come from the Lord, and so far as the angels receive these into themselves, they are in heaven.

Each angel realises implicitly that without the Lord he would neither want to do good nor be able to do good. He disregards his own thoughts and feelings if he sees that they do not come from the Lord. The highest angels of all perceive this and even feel it as a powerful sensation, and the more they do, the more they feel themselves to be in heaven. This is because they have such profound understanding and intense joy. Angels know that life itself can only come from the Lord. They say that nothing can come into existence by itself but only from something that precedes it. Everything exists from a first source whom the angels call the Being of life. It follows that everything continues to exist from this source, because existence is a continual coming into being. If this flow of life were to halt for even a single moment, everything would immediately cease to exist. Angels say that there is but one fountain of life from which all life proceeds. Those who accept this find heaven in themselves but those who deny it or suppress it enter hell and turn life into death.

The angels support this truth by pointing to the way in which the created world mirrors and shows the nature of this inflowing source of life. And because they believe all this, they shrug off any gratitude given them for the good they do. And if they are called 'good' they grow indignant and move away.

Any spirit who believes in his own goodness and who takes the credit for what he does cannot be part of heaven. The angels see him as no more than a foolish thief. In John's gospel, chapter 15, the Lord likens those in heaven to being in him and he in them. The Lord, then, dwells in what is of himself with the angels.

THE DIVINE LIFE IN HEAVEN IS LOVE FOR THE LORD AND ONE'S NEIGHBOUR

Love and truth flow into heaven from the Lord in the same way that heat and light come from the sun. These latter are distinct but they unite to bring life to the earth. In the same way, the Lord's love and truth give life to heaven, because fire is an image of love, and light is an image of truth which comes from love.

Love is what joins people together, so love is what makes heaven. Love joins the angels to the Lord and to each other so that they are seen as one in the Lord's sight. Love is also the substance of life and both angels and people have their lives from it. This can be seen in the warmth and vitality of a loving or loved person and in his coldness when love is absent. Everyone's life is of the same quality as his love.

There are two quite distinct loves in heaven; love for the Lord and love for one's neighbour. Those whose love is focused primarily on the Lord are in the centre of heaven. Those whose love shows itself more in terms of the neighbour are further from the centre. Both these loves come from the Lord and each one makes heaven. In heaven, it is well-known that loving the Lord does not

15

simply mean adoring him as a person but means loving the good which comes from him. And to love his good means to intend doing it and to do it from love. In the same way, love for one's neighbour does not mean loving the person as such, but rather loving the truth and good by which he lives, which come from the Word with him, and as a result intending it and doing it.

The angels go on to describe how these two loves show themselves by a person wanting to do what someone else wants and actually doing it for them. In this way he is loved in return and is joined to him. They also say that the good which comes from the Lord is in the Lord's own likeness and that those who make this good the very principle of their life become likenesses of the Lord and are joined to him. This love even shows itself in the appearance of the angels which is extremely beautiful — the beauty coming from the Lord's influence on them. Love shines on their faces, in their speech and through every action. There are spiritual spheres around each angel which come from their quality of love and these spheres can be recognised even at a distance. The spheres are so full of love that they touch the very depths in other people.

In the spiritual world each spirit turns himself in the direction of his own love. Those who love the Lord and their neighbour continually turn toward the Lord while those who love themselves continually turn away from him. This turning applies to each movement of the body because in heaven space is to do with one's inner state, and direction is according to the focus of one's thought. Nevertheless, it is not the angels who turn toward the Lord but the Lord who turns them toward himself if they love to do the things that come from him.

The reason that love itself is the divine life of heaven is that love contains everything heavenly within it: peace, intelligence, wisdom and happiness. Love seeks to be enriched and perfected and it gladly receives everything with which it is in harmony. This can be seen in the way in which a person's love searches deeply into the memory and draws from it everything that is in agreement with the love, gathering and sorting it out for use and rejecting anything that is discordant. People who have had a simple desire to do what is good during their lives in the world can become very wise after death because they have acquired the means of receiving heaven. On the other hand, selfish and worldly-minded people become progressively ignorant after death and shrink in abhorrence from what is good. Eventually these take themselves off towards hell where they join up with those who are similar to themselves.

HEAVEN HAS TWO DISTINCT KINGDOMS

Heaven is made up of an infinite variety and diversity because no two angels are identical. It is therefore distinguished into different parts which go to make up the whole. Heaven is God's kingdom and is divided into two distinct parts — both of which are then distinguished into three different degrees. There are also countless different communities or groupings of angels.

Some angels are aware of the Lord at a deeper level than others and in a different way. This fact leads to a basic distinction between the two heavenly kingdoms which can be called the 'celestial' and the 'spiritual' kingdoms. Celestial-type angels perceive the truth from the Lord immediately into their life rather than through the memory or reasoning-processes as the spiritual-type angels do. Celestial angels have the truth, as it were, written in their hearts. Being perceptive, they immediately know whether something is true or not and when they hear the truth, they desire to put it to use. Spiritual angels need to reflect and use their reasoning faculties in order to know whether something is true. Because of this basic distinction between them, the two types of angels do not mix freely with each other and they communicate by means of certain intermediate angel communities so that, although heaven has two distinct kingdoms, it nevertheless makes a whole.

HEAVEN HAS THREE DISTINCT DEGREES

Heaven can also be distinguished into three different degrees; a highest degree, or inmost; an intermediate or second degree, and a lowest, outermost or third degree. These may be usefully compared to a house with three storeys.

The mind of a person is arranged in a similar structure because it is also created by the Lord and contains the same divine order and design. So each person is in the heavenly form on the smallest scale. This is how each person can be in communication with the heavens at a deeper level. After death, a person comes to be among angels from one of the three degrees according to the way in which he received the Lord during his earthly life.

The three degrees of heaven are called celestial, spiritual and natural degrees from the ways in which they receive the Lord. The natural, or lowest degree of heaven, also has what are either celestial or spiritual types of angels within it, so that it is more accurate to talk of a celestial-natural degree and a spiritual-natural degree.

In each heavenly degree there are some angels who have a deeper awareness than others. This degree of perception leads an angel to be nearer the centre or further towards the circumference of the particular degree of heaven in which he is. The more an angel's mind is opened towards the Lord, the more central his position will be in the heaven in which he is.

Those angels who are moved by the truth and who want to make immediate use of it are in the highest or inmost degree of heaven. Those angels who take the truth into their memory and so into their understanding, and from there want to make use of it, are in the second or intermediate degree. And those who live decent, upright lives and believe in a divine being but who don't care much for learning, are in the third or outermost degree.

Heavenly perception increases as one moves more towards the centre or to what is highest, because this is nearer to the Divine. Angelic perfection lies in intelligence, wisdom and love, and the happiness that comes from these. The angels of the inmost heaven are more attuned to the Lord than the angels in the other two degrees; therefore their perfection is greater.

These distinctions of degree mean that angels from one heaven do not easily associate with those from another. If an angel ascends from a lower heaven to a higher, he begins to feel distressed. He is unable to see those who are there or to talk with them.

If an angel descends from a higher heaven to a lower, he

loses his wisdom, stammers, and eventually has to take his leave. The Lord does permit occasional exceptions as, for example, when an angel is allowed to see the glory of a higher heaven for his own benefit. But such angels are carefully prepared in advance and are surrounded by special intermediate angels through whom there is perfect communication.

Angels who are in the same heaven can mix freely with all who are there and enjoy being together so long as they have similar affections.

Even though these distinctions exist, still the heavens as a whole make a one because of the Lord and also because one heaven influences another. In these ways, the three heavens make one so that throughout, nothing is unconnected.

It is essential to understand how these degrees operate in spiritual things in order to have a clear idea of the form of heaven. People tend to think of degrees in terms of gradual changes, such as from darkness to light or from heat to cold, but spiritual degrees operate in another, more discrete way. From one level or degree comes another, which is different yet connected, like cause and effect, and from this comes a third. The two that emerge are contained within the first, just as a person's mind and body are the product of his spirit but are not themselves part of it. If this principle is not grasped, there can be no understanding of many things, such as the heavenly form, the human mind, the relationship between the spiritual and natural worlds, nor the nature and origin of correspondence. Every single angel and person has an innermost or highest degree of all where the Lord's life flows in directly. By means of this, the Lord arranges everything else into its subsequent and proper order. This is the soul itself, which is the Lord's very own 'dwelling place' with each person. It is this level that makes a person truly human, unlike the animals who do not have this level within them at all. It is because of this level that a person can be raised by the Lord into the light of heaven, can believe in the Lord, can be moved by him and see him. By means of this level a person can have intelligence and reasoning, and finally is able to live for ever. Yet all the time there is no awareness of its existence because it belongs to the Lord alone.

HEAVEN IS MADE UP OF COUNTLESS COMMUNITIES

In each of the three degrees of heaven, the angels are grouped into varying-sized communities each of which reflects the particular qualities of those who are there. Those who have similar qualities form one community together and because there are infinite varieties of good qualities, there are countless communities.

The heavenly communities are situated in relation to one another according to the difference in their particular qualities of good. This is due to the fact that distances in the spiritual world are the result of variations in inner states. People who differ greatly are far apart; those who differ less are closer together, and similarity brings proximity.

Again, those who are within the same community are arranged similarly. The more perfect ones are to be found nearer to the centre; the less perfect towards the circumference, according to the degree of perfection. In each case, the arrangement within the community can be compared to the way that light diminishes as it passes further from the source of light towards the boundaries. Those who are at the centre are in the greatest light. One of the universal laws of heaven is that like is attracted to like. People who are with others like themselves feel at home, as if they were with their own family, and they feel free, at peace and intensely happy.

It may be seen, then, that it is the quality of good that joins the heavens as a whole and also that people are distinguished by their particular quality of good. Still, it is not the angels who do the arranging, but the Lord who is the source of good. He leads, joins, distinguishes and brings freedom, keeping everyone in the life of their particular love, faith and joy.

People who have a similar kind of good recognise each other in heaven in the same way people on earth recognise members of their own family, relatives and friends. This happens even though they may never have seen each other before. The only relationships in heaven are spiritual ones, which are to do with love and faith. I have seen this for myself. Some angels I saw seemed to have known me from my childhood, while others appeared not to know me. Those who seemed to know me were in a similar spiritual state to mine.

Angels who live in the same community generally look alike, but not in a detailed way. They resemble each other because the quality of their love shines on their faces and even forms the features. I saw the face of an angel and I saw, as a kind of demonstration to me, how its expression changed to show all the various types of affection there can be in one single heavenly community. This lasted some time, and I noticed that the same general face was there all the time as a background, even through the expression kept changing. Angels can immediately see what another angel is like by looking at his face. In heaven it is impossible for anyone to hide how he is feeling or what he is thinking, or to pretend to be other than he is.

All the communities in heaven are in touch with each other but not by any direct exchange, since few people go from their own community to another one. This would be like leaving oneself and going somewhere else that doesn't feel right. Instead, they are in touch by means of the spheres which come from them and which can extend far and wide, affecting others very deeply. In this manner, the angels of the highest heaven have a strong influence through heaven as a whole, as their sphere pervades everywhere. And it is by the effect of these spheres that in heaven each angel is in communication with everyone else there, and everyone with each.

There are larger and smaller communities of angels in heaven, made up of myriads, or of thousands, or of some hundreds of angels. And there are also some who live apart from others, house by house, or family by family, as it were. Although these are spread out, they are still in an orderly arrangement just like the people in communities. These people are more directly under the Lord's sight and guidance and they are the best angels of all.

EACH COMMUNITY IS A HEAVEN
IN MINIATURE AND EACH ANGEL
IS A HEAVEN ON THE SMALLEST SCALE OF ALL

As it is the quality of good that makes heaven, so this quality is within every heavenly community and also in each angel. It does not matter that this good varies, it is still heavenly good. The difference is just that heaven is of one kind in one place and of another kind in another place.

Each heavenly community is a miniature heaven because the same pattern is there as in heaven as a whole. Those nearer to the centre are more spiritual while those who are less spiritual are grouped around in decreasing order towards the circumference. This shows how the Lord guides everyone who is in heaven as though they were one angel. He does the same with those in each community. An angelic community can sometimes take on the appearance of being as if one angel.

Because of this great diversity throughout the whole of heaven, there is a wide variety of ways in which angels respond to the Lord; for instance, in the different ways they worship him. All this is in the divine order of things because the very perfection of heaven lies in its increasing variety. The principle can be put like this: that for something to be perfect, it has to be formed from various diverse parts. We can see that this is so from the way beauty, pleasantness and delight move our senses and bring the feeling of perfection, from the harmony of everything in agreement. This, for us, is a kind of mirror in which we can see something of heaven. Indeed, what happens in this world here is a mirror of things in the spiritual world.

The same is true of the Church; for, although there are many, each one may be a Church if the quality of good is in it. The same is also true of any individual person in the Church. He is a 'church' in miniature. There is virtually no difference between this sort of person and an angel in whom heaven is present. Both of them are forms of heaven on the smallest scale of all. The Lord created people so that

24

they may come into heaven and become angels. One who has good from the Lord is an 'angelic person'. But there is this difference between them; that while a person's inner form is in the heavenly pattern, like an angel's, his outer form is shaped according to the pattern of the world. He has this level over and above what angels have, and so far as he is in good, this worldly level is subordinated to heaven and serves it. Then the Lord is present with him on both levels, just as if he were in heaven.

Lastly, it is worth noting that the person who has heaven in himself has it not only in the most important things or the general things about him but also in every small detail of his life. These repeat the pattern of the greatest things as in an image. This is because in heaven every person is in the form of his own love, which flows into everything he is and arranges it into its pattern. As it is love to the Lord that makes heaven, so the Lord flows into each and all things, clothing them with his own likeness and bringing heaven wherever he is.

HEAVEN AS A WHOLE
RESEMBLES THE HUMAN FORM

The angels call heaven the 'Great Human'. This is universally understood by the angels who know that the heavens as a whole, including their own communities, resemble the form of a single person. Many important ideas follow from this concept and they cannot be clearly seen without understanding this concept.

It is possible to think of a person purely in physical terms when yet a person is what he is from being able to understand true ideas and wanting to do good. The physical body is there simply to serve these inner faculties and it is subservient to them. It does nothing of itself.

This is the way that angels think about a person. They disregard what a person is doing with his body and concentrate instead on the desires and intentions that lie behind the action. They call this level the person himself. No single angel sees heaven in its entirety because this is beyond comprehension. From time to time, however, an angel can see a complete community that is made up of many thousands of angels and they see it in the form a single person. They deduce from this that the whole of the heavens resembles the human form, not in its shape but in its organisation.

Since heaven is in this human form, it is governed by the Lord as though it were one single person, as an entity, in the same way that all the organs and cells of the physical body work together as one when a person does something. Every part of the body contributes to its welfare and each part has its own special use. The whole body provides what each part requires, and the various parts of the body provide in specific ways for the whole body. In this mutual service lies the unity. In heaven there is the same pattern of organisation which is according to the use that is provided. Usefulness is to seek the welfare of others for the sake of the good of all; and everyone in heaven looks first to the Lord as the source, and then to his kingdom as the community whose welfare is to be sought.

As heaven resembles the organisation of the physical body, it is similarly arranged into various members and parts and these have the same names. Angels know which communities form part of the 'head', the 'breasts', the 'loins' of heaven, and so on. Generally speaking, it is the highest heavens that form the head down to the neck, the middle or second heavens that form the breast down to the loins and knees, and the lowest or third heavens that form the feet down to the soles, and the arms to the fingertips, for these are the outermost things in a person.

These principles that concern the 'Great Human' are essential knowledge if a true idea of heaven and the way it is linked with people is to be grasped.

EACH COMMUNITY IN HEAVEN RESEMBLES THE HUMAN FORM

Each heavenly community appears in the form of a single person when the Lord is present in it. The more that any discordant element is removed, the more clearly this is seen. Yet no single community is exactly like another. They differ just as the faces of people in the same family differ, and are according to the varieties of good which determine the form as a whole. The people in each community, making it appear to be like a single person, are the ones who are involved in the particular good of that community. The communities that are in the centre of the highest heavens have the most perfect and beautiful form of all. The more people there are in one community, the more perfect its form becomes, because it has increasing variety. As a result, heaven as a whole is being made more perfect as its numbers increase daily. Angels like nothing better than the arrival of new angel guests among them.

EACH ANGEL IS A COMPLETE HUMAN FORM

A single angel is a miniature of heaven because in him there is the image of the whole and the parts. Heaven is a communion of angels because it shares everything of itself with each angel, and each angel receives all that he has from the whole communion of heaven. So each angel is a receiver and therefore a miniature heaven. Many people have the mistaken idea that spirits are nothing but disembodied thoughts and feelings but I have never seen anything to suggest this to be so from all my own experience in the spiritual world. I have met individual spirits and groups of spirits and spoken to them and I have seen nothing about them which is different from that of a person. People who have a simple and clear faith always think of angels as being people, because they are not caught up in the wrong idea, nor are they able to think of anything that has no form or substance to it.

Angels are people in every sense, and they have faces, ears, eyes, bodies, hands and feet, just as people do. They see and hear each other, and they talk among themselves. They lack nothing that a person has, except for one difference; instead of having a material body, angels have a spiritual body that is made of spiritual substance.

We need to appreciate that people can't see angels by means of their physical senses but only through the eyes of the spirit. This level is in the spiritual world, while everything physical is in the natural world. Like sees like because it is made of similar substance. If the physical eyes are incapable of seeing so many things in nature, how much less will they be able to see the things of the spiritual world?

And yet these become visible to a person when he is withdrawn from physical sight and his spiritual sight is opened.

HEAVEN AS A WHOLE AND IN PART RESEMBLES THE HUMAN FORM BECAUSE IT COMES FROM THE LORD'S DIVINE HUMAN

Everything that has been said so far stems from the all-important truth that the Divine of the Lord is Human in form because it is this that makes heaven. Angels cannot think about the Divine in any other way at all. They think like this because they are guided both by the Divine itself which flows into them and because of the form of heaven according to which their thoughts reach out all around them. The wiser angels are, the more clearly they understand this to be true; and as a result of this perception, the Lord appears to them. The Lord actually appears as an 'Angel' in human form to people who acknowledge and believe in a visible Divine but not to people who believe in an invisible Divine. The former can see the Divine; the latter cannot.

The angels go on to say that only the Lord is 'Person', and that they themselves are people because of him. They add that each of them is a person only to the degree that he receives the Lord. This is seen from the appearance of the angels from the highest heaven who receive the Lord in themselves the most of all. They are the most beautiful angels of all because understanding and wisdom form the real person.

Every person who receives any influence from heaven thinks of God as being in human form, because this is how God is perceived in heaven. But people who only think from themselves destroy this idea, and they can only think of God as invisible. People who have chosen to lead an evil way of life think that there is no God at all. No-one can enter heaven without some concept of the Divine.

Without any idea of the Divine, no spirit could even approach the very threshold of heaven. Were he to come near it, he would feel a resistance from within, because his inner mind is closed up and not in the heavenly form.

The worldly-minded person has difficulty in understanding this idea of God as a 'Person'. His whole outlook is based only on what his senses tell him, and on the appearance of space round about him. There isn't a fixed extension of space in heaven as there is in the world — distance there not being like distance here — instead there is boundless space, because it comes from inner sight or thought, which has no bounds. In heaven, everything is communicated to each individual, because this is the way in which thought works.

THERE IS A CORRESPONDING RELATIONSHIP BETWEEN EVERYTHING IN HEAVEN AND EVERYTHING HUMAN

The nature of the relationship which exists between heaven and what is human is unknown today, and for several reasons. The main reason is that people have withdrawn themselves from heaven by loving themseves and the world. This tends to make a person concentrate on worldly things that appeal to his physical senses, and which delight him, and he then overlooks spiritual things, dismissing them as too abstract to think about.

People in very ancient times felt differently about such things. They believed that an understanding of this relationship — or correspondence — between heaven and what is human was the noblest knowledge of all. It made them wise and it gave them their understanding, and they were in communication with heaven by it, because it is an angelic knowledge.

This present ignorance of such things makes it impossible for people to know about the spiritual world, or the way in which it affects the natural world and human life. Nor can man's spirit or soul be understood, in the way in which it acts on the body, nor anything about a person's life after death, without this essential knowledge. Because this is so, the nature of the relationship needs to be explained in order to clear the way for further matters.

First, the nature of correspondence itself. Everything in the natural world exists from the spiritual world, just as an effect comes from the cause that produces it. Because of this, everything in the natural world has a correspondence to or is an image of something in the spiritual world. Since a person is both a heaven in miniature and also a world in miniature, he has a spiritual world and a natural world within him. Everything that occurs on the level of his natural world — his body, its senses and its actions — comes into being from his spiritual world — his mind, its understanding and what it intends — and the two are in correspondence.

A person's face illustrates this admirably. In an open face that does not simulate or feign affection, the true thoughts and feelings of the person become clearly visible. This is why the face is called the index of the mind; it is a person's spiritual world contained within his natural world. Now to move on to the correspondence of heaven as a whole with everything of a person. Heaven reflects the form of a person because it is organised and arranged in the human form or 'Great Human'. The communities that

31

make heaven are arranged like the parts of the body, some in the head, some in the breast, some in the arms, some in specific parts of these, and so on. Communities in a particular part of the 'Great Human' correspond to the same part in the person himself, for example, those in the head correspond to the head of a person. The importance of this link or relationship is that a person has his existence here from this correspondence, since man only exists from the inflow of heaven.

The two general kingdoms of heaven have already been described. The celestial kingdom corresponds overall to the heart and to everything concerned with the heart throughout the body. The spiritual kingdom corresponds overall to the lungs in the same way. The heart and lungs make two kingdoms in a person, the heart acting through the arteries and veins, the lungs affecting the nerves and the muscles. They are both involved in every physical effort or movement. In the same way there are two overall kingdoms in each person's spiritual make-up, in his intention and also in his understanding. The intention acts through a love for what is good while the understanding acts through a love of what is true. These correspond to the heart and lungs in the body.

It is just the same in heaven as a whole. The celestial kingdom, where love rules, is the intention part of heaven, and the spiritual kingdom, where truth rules, is the understanding part of heaven. These correspond as well to the heart and lungs in the body. This correspondence shows why the 'heart', when mentioned in the Bible, stands for the things of love, and also why the 'breath' stands for the things of the understanding. It also shows why affections are said to be of the heart, even though they are not in or from the heart.

This is also the reason why parts of the body are mentioned in the Bible to stand for spiritual things, because everything in the Bible also has this correspondence. The 'head' is used to mean understanding and wisdom; the 'breast' to mean love and affection; the 'loins' marriage love; the 'arms' and the 'hands' the power of what is true; the 'feet' what is natural; the 'eyes' understanding; the 'nostrils' perception; the 'ears' obedience; the 'kidneys' the examination of what is true, and so on.

Even in everyday speech, people talk about a 'good head' to mean intelligence, about a 'bosom friend' or 'having a keen nose' or being 'sharp-sighted'. All these expressions come from this correspondence; in fact, they originate from the spiritual world, although this isn't realised.

Even though everything to do with a person's physical body corresponds to something of heaven, still a person is not a representation of heaven as far as his outer form is concerned but only as far as his inner form is concerned. It is this level that receives heaven; the outward body only receives from the world.

So man's physical body is where the heavenly form finally rests; it is what heaven stands on as a base. But it must be appreciated that all the correspondence of the body with heaven is because of the Lord's 'Divine Human', since heaven is from him and he is heaven. This explains why the Lord came into the world as a man. This happened because the 'Divine Human' which was keeping heaven in its order before the Lord came was no longer sufficient to preserve heaven because people, who are the base of heaven, had weakened and destroyed the pattern.

HEAVEN ALSO CORRESPONDS
TO EVERYTHING IN NATURE

Everything in the natural world corresponds to something of the spiritual world because natural things have their existence from spiritual causes, and both come from the Divine. Everything on earth is divided into the three kingdoms — animal, vegetable and mineral. Each kingdom corresponds in general to a different level of the spiritual world and each kingdom contains the various things that have a specific correspondence. In a word, everything in nature, from the smallest to the greatest, is in correspondence. As illustration of this, take the fact that in the animal kingdom there are many creatures which have instinctive knowledge. For example, bees know how to gather honey, how to store it by building cells, and how to provide food for themselves and for their young against the coming winter. They live in an orderly pattern which they have instinctively.

In the vegetable kingdom there is the example of the growth of seeds into trees which produce leaves, and bear flowers and then fruit in which new seeds are contained. These developments happen in an orderly sequence, occurring together in such a marvellous order that any full description is impossible.

In general, animals correspond to various affections — the gentler and more useful animals to good affections, the fierce animals to evil ones. Cows and calves in particular correspond to natural affections in a person's mind that are to do with usefulness, while lambs correspond to spiritual affections. On the other hand, the many different kinds of birds correspond to levels of thought in the mind, both natural thoughts and spiritual thoughts. The same is true of things in the vegetable and mineral kingdoms. The link between heaven and earth is by means of these correspondences. It works in the following way: The Lord's kingdom is a kingdom of useful purpose, and the entire universe is created in such a way that wherever there is a use it can be clothed in the kind of form that enables it to fulfil the Lord's purpose in creating it. This principle operates first in heaven and then in the created world, even down to the physical substances of nature itself.

The correspondence between what is spiritual and what is natural — or between heaven and earth — is through use, which itself makes the connection. The various forms that clothe these uses are correspondences, and they make the link to the extent that they are the form of the particular use.

LIFE IN HEAVEN

THE SUN IN HEAVEN

The sun of this world is not seen in heaven at all because it is purely natural. Yet even so, there is still a sun in heaven, just as there is also light and warmth. The sun of heaven is the Lord. The light of heaven is divine truth, and the warmth there is divine good, issuing from the Lord as if from a sun. The reason the Lord is the sun of heaven is that he is divine love, the source of everything spiritual. It is this love which shines in heaven like a sun.

Since the Lord then is visible in heaven as a sun — because of his divine love which is both in him and flows from him — therefore all people in heaven turn towards him all the time. But people in the hells turn towards the darkness that is hell, and so turn their backs to the Lord. This turning takes place because people in the other life look to what inwardly motivates them, which is their own loves. In the spiritual world there are no fixed points of the compass as there are in this world; it is the focus that determines direction there.

People also, in spirit, turn themselves similarly in this world. Those who are motivated by self-love and worldly loves turn themselves away from the Lord, whereas those who love the Lord and their neighbour turn towards him. But because people live in a world of fixed points of the compass, they are unaware of this fact.

And because the Lord is the sun of heaven and everything that comes from him turns towards him, the Lord is the centre of all and the source of every direction and purpose. So too everything that is beneath is in his presence and under his guidance, both in heaven and on earth.

LIGHT AND HEAT IN HEAVEN

People who only think about things from nature cannot possibly understand that there is light in heaven which is indeed far brighter than the light of the midday sun. This isn't a natural light at all, as the world's light is, but a spiritual light. It actually comes from the Lord as the sun, this sun being divine love from which divine truth comes forth as light. Truth is light to the angels because they are spiritual beings who perceive things from the light of their sun. Angels understand everything about life from divine truth, and their understanding is an inner sight which flows into their outer sight and produces it.

As this is the source of light in heaven, then this light varies according to the way in which divine truth is received from the Lord and according to the degree of intelligence and wisdom with the angels. There is a different kind of light in the celestial kingdom than there is in the spiritual kingdom and it is also different within each community and with each individual.

The light of heaven reveals everything as it really is. Nothing is in the least bit concealed. The higher angels love to reveal themselves openly because they have only good intentions, but those who are below heaven are very afraid of being seen in the light of heaven. And strange as it may seem, people in hell look quite human to each other but when they are seen in the light of heaven they look like monsters with frightful faces and bodies which are the actual forms of their own evil. The same is true of people in the world when angels see their spiritual state. If they are inwardly good, they look like beautiful people, but if they are inwardly evil, they look like deformed monsters.

Heat — or warmth — in heaven is love which comes from the Lord as the sun because he is divine love. Like light, it is variously received in heaven according to the degree of love within each community of angels. Goodness, which is love, and truth, which is light, come from the Lord as a single emanation because they are truly one, but the angels see them to be distinct because some angels receive more of one than of the other. The most perfect angels are those who receive both to the same extent.

THE FOUR REGIONS OF HEAVEN

In heaven, as in the world, there are four main regions: east, south, west and north. In the world these are determined by the positions of the sun, but in heaven they result from the presence of the Lord. The direction in which the Lord is seen as the sun is called the 'east'. The opposite direction is 'west'; 'south' is to the right, and 'north' is to the left. This holds true no matter which way people turn their faces or their bodies because in heaven all directions are determined from the east. The direction in which the Lord is seen is called the 'east' because he is the source of life, and to the extent that warmth and light — which are love and understanding — are received by angels, the Lord is said to have risen among them. The east is also continually in front of angels, whichever way they may turn their faces or their bodies. The angels turn in a different way from that of people on earth because their reason for turning is different. They turn to what they love, and as a result their love is continually before them. In heaven, the Lord is the source of their love, and since the Lord is with them in his love, he causes them to behold him no matter in which direction they face.

As a result of this, a remarkable situation occurs in heaven. Many people there can be in one place, one turning his face and body this way and another in another way, and yet all of them will see the Lord in front of them. And each will have the south to his right, the north to his left, and the west behind him. For another remarkable fact in heaven is that, even though the angels face towards the east, they still have a view towards the other three regions. This comes from their more inward sight which is to do with thought.

People in heaven live in different areas according to these four regions. The people who are involved in the things of love and goodness live to the east and west — those who are more perceptive being to the east, and those less so being to the west — while people who are in the light of wisdom live to the south, and those with less light live to the north. This arrangement is true both of heaven as a whole and within each single community. In general, communities that are towards the east are better than those towards the west, and those towards the south are better than the ones towards the north.

CHANGING STATES OF ANGELS IN HEAVEN

By this is meant a change — or alteration — in the things of love, wisdom and understanding with the angels, and so also in their own states of life. Angels do not remain in the same state continually but pass through various changes. Each angel's love and wisdom varies according to his particular state at the time. Sometimes the angels feel intensely loving, at other times they feel less loving. This intensity varies by degrees from greatest to least. When they feel most loving they are in the fullest light and warmth of their love. When they feel less love they are in relative cold or shade, even to being in an obscure or unpleasant state. Yet they return from these to the first stage and these changes follow on from one another, like the daily cycle of light and shade, warmth and cold, and morning and evening as in the world. These things actually correspond. Morning corresponds to angelic love when it is in its full strength, noon corresponds to their wisdom when it is in greatest light, evening to love and wisdom in relative shade, and night to the absence of any love or wisdom. Note however that night itself has no correspondence with the states of people in heaven, but only with those who are in hell. In heaven, the 'evening' state leads to daybreak which precedes the coming new morning.

As well as changes in their inner states, there are also changes in the appearance of the different things that angels see around them. These will be explained in due course.

The reasons for all these changes can be shown. The angels say that there is need for continual variety in spiritual life. Their appreciation of heaven would gradually diminish if it were always the same, in the same way that people here who indulge in pleasures and comforts with no respite lose the feeling of delight in these things. Another reason for change is that angels, like people here, have self-awareness. There is a tendency because of this to think of themselves too much at times. Everyone in heaven is kept

41

away from this power of self-love. So far as they are kept from it by the Lord they experience the things of love and wisdom, but so far as they become immersed in it — or are let into it — they experience self-love.

A third reason is that these changes help the angels become more perfect. These changing states make their perception and their awareness of what is good more sensitive. They are the means by which angels grow used to the feeling of having love to the Lord and of being kept from self-love.

TIME IN HEAVEN

In spite of the fact that everything in heaven happens in sequence and progresses in the same way that things do in the world, angels have no real concept of time and space. This is so much so that they do not understand what these are as such. Time in our world is based on the apparent movement of the sun, producing times and seasons. The sun of heaven does not produce days and years by such a sequence nor by any orbital movement, but it appears to bring about changes of state which do not happen at fixed intervals. This is why angels have no concept of time but only of passing states, and they understand everything that is to do with time in this way. Since angels have no idea of time, their understanding of what eternity means is quite different from that of people. Angels see eternity to mean an infinite state and not an infinite length of time. If one thinks only in terms of time, space and matter, thought becomes limited, but if it goes beyond these things on to a higher plane of thought, it can expand without limit.

REPRESENTATIONS AND APPEARANCES IN HEAVEN

There is no simple way to describe how angels in heaven see the things that are around them. Let it just be said that they are rather like things that are in the world, but more perfect and more abundant. That there really are objects and things in heaven is confirmed by what the Biblical prophets saw in their visions. These things became visible to the prophets when heaven was opened to them, which happens when the more inward or spiritual sight is opened. Heavenly things cannot be seen by means of a person's physical eyes but only by his spiritual eyes. These are opened, when the Lord permits it, as the person is taken out of his natural perception which is from the physical senses and raised into spiritual light and understanding.

Even so, heavenly things, while they are generally the same as things on earth, are quite different in many ways. A basic difference is that things in heaven exist from the spiritual sun, while the things on earth exist from the sun of this world. Things in heaven do not occur in the same way as things on earth do. In heaven, everything comes from the Lord, according to its correspondence with the states of angels there. Since everything in heaven that corresponds to inner states actually re-presents them, they are called 'representations' of them. And because things in heaven also vary according to the states of angels, they are called 'appearances'. This is so in spite of the fact that things in heaven are perfectly visible and seen to be just as real as things in this world. In heaven, objects are seen much more clearly then they are here.

The appearances that occur in heaven are called 'real appearances' because they really do occur. There are also

43

unreal appearances, which are things that become visible but which do not correspond to more inward things.

Here is just one example which illustrates the kind of things that angels see as a result of correspondence: Parks and gardens which are full of trees and flowers appear in front of and around intelligent angels, and they are arranged in perfect order. There are arched entrances and pathways here and there. People who stroll there are full of understanding. They pick the flowers and make garlands from them which they then put on little children. There are trees and flowers there that are unknown in this world, and the fruit on the trees represents the goodness in the love these angels have. They see this kind of scene because parks and gardens, fruit trees and flowers correspond to intelligence and wisdom.

THE CLOTHES OF ANGELS IN HEAVEN

The angels have clothes because they are people who live together just as people on earth do. They also have houses and similar things. But there is a distinct difference; everything that they have is more perfect because they are in a more perfect state. Since angelic wisdom far surpasses human wisdom, so too does everything perceived in heaven. Angels' clothes correspond, just as everything else does in heaven, and because they correspond, they actually exist. Their clothes correspond to their intelligence. People in heaven are seen dressed in keeping with their intelligence, and because one person surpasses another in intelligence, so one will have finer clothes than another. The clothes of the most intelligent angels gleam as though they are on fire; the less intelligent have shining white clothes, and those still less intelligent have clothes of different colours. The best angels of all go naked.

Because angels' clothes correspond to their ingelligence, the garments themselves correspond to particular truths, as all intelligence comes from divine truth. It makes no real difference whether you say that angels are dressed in keeping with intelligence or in keeping with divine truth.

The appearance of flaming clothes and shining garments comes from the correspondence of fire to love, and light to what is true. The extent of these appearances is in proportion to the reception of the Lord by the angels. The clothes of various colours, likewise, correspond to diffe-rent kinds of reception. The reason that the best angels are naked is because only they are in innocence, and inno-cence is represented in nakedness. The angels not only see these clothes but they can also feel them. In addition, they have a number of clothes which they put on and take off, put away and take out again to wear. They say that these clothes are given to them from the Lord, and that at times they are clothed without knowing it.

Because clothes in the spiritual world are always in keeping with the qualities of the people there, those people who are in hell, who do not want to know the truth, are seen to be dressed in torn, dirty, or even offensive clothes, each in keeping with his insanity. They are unable to wear anything else. The Lord gives them their clothes so that they may not be seen naked.

HOUSES AND HOMES IN HEAVEN

Angels live together in communities, and therefore they have their own houses and homes which, like their clothes, vary according to the individual quality of their lives. There are magnificent houses for those angels in a higher state, and less elaborate ones for those who are in

45

lower states. Their dwellings are just like those on earth that are called homes, except that they are more beautiful. They have rooms, suites and bedrooms in large number. There are courtyards which are surrounded by gardens, flowerbeds and lawns.

Where people live in close proximity, the houses are next to each other, arranged like a city with avenues, streets, and squares like cities in this world. The design of the buildings in heaven is so perfect that you would say they represent the very essence of the art, and no wonder, since the art of architecture itself comes from heaven. Angels say that the Lord puts these beautiful things — and other still more perfect things — there before their eyes. Yet these things are in fact more pleasing to their minds than to their eyes because they see correspondences in everything, and through these they see divine things.

Even the different things that are in the houses correspond. The house itself broadly corresponds to the good of those who live there and the particular things inside it correspond to the various qualities that go to make that good. Outside the houses are the things that correspond to the truths that arise from this good, and also to perceptions and insights.

The homes of angels are not built in the way that houses are built in the world but they are freely given to angels by the Lord, to everyone in accordance with his reception of what is good and true. Everything that the angels possess they hold as gifts from the Lord and they are given whatever they need.

SPACE IN HEAVEN

Although everything in heaven appears to be in a place and in space just like things are in the world, angels have no notion of place and space. This must seem like a paradox, so it needs to be explained clearly.

A change of place in the spiritual world comes about by means of inner changes of state so that changes of place — or travelling — are simply changes of state. This is how all the angels travel. They do not have distance or space for movement because they exist in another dimension which is that of state.

As this is how changes of place happen in heaven, it is clear that those people who are in a similar state are near to one another, while people in differing states are further apart, for what is similar is close and what is dissimilar is distant. There are no spaces in heaven except outward states that correspond to inner ones. It is for this reason that the kingdoms and degrees of heaven are distinct from each other, also the communities in each heaven, and also the individual angels in each community. This is also the reason that hell is completely separate from heaven, since they are in opposite states.

This is the reason too that in the spiritual world any person who longs to be with someone else comes into his presence, because he thinks about the other person and so puts himself in his state. On the other hand, a person is removed from another person so far as he turns away from him. Since this turning away arises from discordant thoughts, it happens that, when several people are in one place, they can be seen so long as they agree. But the moment they disagree, they vanish.

When anyone goes from one place to another, he gets

there more quickly if he wants to be there and more slowly if he doesn't. The journey itself becomes longer or shorter accordingly, even though it is the same distance.

THE FORM OF HEAVEN WHICH SETS THE PATTERN FOR ALL ITS ASSOCIATION AND COMMUNICATION

To some extent, the overall organisation of heaven can be seen from what has been said about it so far. The point is, that it is this form which makes the pattern for all its groupings and all communication there. Not only this, but it is also the pattern for all outgoing thoughts and affection and all the intelligence and wisdom of the angels. The extent to which a person is in the heavenly form determines how wise he is. This heavenly form depends on specific laws of order which operate in the spiritual world. Being in the form of heaven really means living according to this order. A person here is created in the image of heaven, but outwardly he is in the image of the world. Because people have destroyed the heavenly image in them by allowing evil desires and false ideas to enter their minds, the deeper things in a person are closed off from the time he is born. This is the reason why people, unlike animals, are born into complete ignorance. In fact, if the heavenly form is to be restored at all, he needs to be taught about the things of order, because form itself comes from order.

The Bible contains all the laws of divine order in the various commandments given through it. So far as a person knows them and lives by them, the things that are closed up in him are set free. Then the heavenly image is newly formed within him. We can see, therefore, what being in the heavenly form means, namely, living by the things that are there in the Bible.

The way that angels are drawn to each other in groups is based on their spiritual affinity. This is true in heaven as a whole, also in each community, and in each family unit. Angels who are in similar states recognise each other just as relatives do here, and they are drawn to each other, and understand each other's minds very well.

This is the form as it is in each heaven, a form which shapes the sharing of the angels' thoughts and feelings. But there is a different communication between the various heavens, which should be called influence rather than communication. Since the angels are joined together only by the Lord flowing into them, every care is taken lest angels of a higher heaven enter a lower heaven to talk with those who are there. For if this were to happen, the higher angels would immediately lose all their understanding. This would happen because each angel has three levels to his life, just as heaven as a whole has its three levels. Angels in the highest heaven have their highest level of life opened up, and the lower two are closed. Angels in the middle heaven have the second level opened; and angels in the lowest heaven have the lowest level opened and the two higher levels are closed. The moment an angel from the highest heaven were to enter a lower heaven to talk to anyone there, his own level of life would become closed. And once closed, he would lose that wisdom which is only there on the highest level, until he returned.

There is no inflowing from lower to higher heavens because this is contrary to order. Influence always comes from higher to lower heavens.

The wisdom of angels who come from a higher heaven surpasses that of angels in lower heavens by a ratio of about a thousand to one. This is why angels in lower heavens cannot talk with those in higher ones. In fact, they don't even see them when they look at them. Their heaven looks like a mist up above them. On the other hand, angels of a higher heaven can see those in lower heavens, but they are not permitted to talk with them on pain of losing their own level of wisdom, as said before.

THE WAY HEAVEN IS GOVERNED

Since heaven is made up of communities, each one of which may have hundreds of thousands of angels in it, and since those who are in each community are involved in the same kind of good, there is the need for government there. Order must be maintained, and matters of order taken care of.

But there is no government at all in heaven that does not come from mutual love. And the kind of government varies according to what is appropriate to each community: it is not universally the same.

In the celestial kingdom, governments come from the Lord alone who guides and teaches them in the things of life. What is true is there in their hearts, and they all know and understand it straight away. There are never any legal wrangles, only a love for justice. Those who are less wise ask those who are wiser about these things, and the wise enquire of the Lord and receive answers. Their heaven, or what amounts to the same, their greatest joy, is living justly from the Lord.

Those who are in the spiritual kingdom are concerned more with love towards the neighbour and what this involves. This quality is based on the need for truth and understanding in decision-making. These angels are guided by the Lord, but more indirectly. They have officials, the number of which depends on the needs of the community. They also have laws which they keep to harmoniously. The officials govern everything by these laws. They understand them because they are wise, and if they are in any doubt they are enlightened by the Lord.

The various kinds of government in the spiritual kingdom differ from one community to another and have all kinds of functions, just as the parts of the body vary, to which they each correspond. Yet all the forms of government there agree in that they focus on the common good as their objective, and within this to the good of each individual. Everyone is directly under the care of the Lord, and he ensures that the common good be the source from which individuals receive their own good. Each angel receives what is good so far as he loves the whole.

Those who govern are the ones who have the most love and wisdom: the ones who seek the good of all and who know how to provide for it. People who are like this do not want to hold sway over others nor to give orders; they minister and serve, which is doing good to others from a love for what is good. They do not make more of themselves than of others, but less, because they give their whole attention to the good of the community and the neighbour. Even so, they are given honour and glory. They live in the centre of the community, higher up than others, and in magnificent houses. They accept this recognition gladly, though not for themselves but out of obedience. Everyone knows perfectly well that this honour is given to them by the Lord and on that account they are to be obeyed. Performing useful tasks is the delight of everyone's life. Obviously then the Lord's kingdom is one of useful occupation.

In appearance, worship in heaven is rather like worship in the world, but inwardly it is quite different. As is the case here, there are services and church buildings, and they use teachings with which the sermons are in keeping. The reason why these things occur in heaven is that angels are continually growing in love and wisdom. Yet worship in heaven is not just a matter of church-going and of listening carefully to the sermon, but it is a life of love, neighbourliness and faith that is based on true teachings. Church services are simply the means of further instruction in matters of life.

The teachings on which all preaching is based are all directly related to life.

None of them separates matters of faith from life. And in each heaven the teachings are given on a level that matches the particular perception of the angels who are there. The essential ingredient in all teachings is the acknowledgement of the Lord's 'Divine Human'.

All the preachers belong to the spiritual kingdom and not to the celestial one. The reason for this is that in the services people are concerned with true ideas that come from what is good, and all preaching is done from truth. However, those who are in the celestial kingdom still have sermons, as by means of them they are given light on the truth that they already know and they are made even more perfect by hearing many truths that are new to them. As soon as they hear them, they see them, love them, and make them part of their life by living by them.

The preacher stands in the pulpit towards the east. Immediately in front of him sit those angels who are in greater light of wisdom, with those in lesser light on their right and left. They are all set out in a circular fashion so that the preacher can see them all. Newcomers sit nearer to the door, towards the east of the church. And no-one sits behind the preacher at all. If there were anyone there, or if anyone were to dissent, the preacher would become confused. All the preachers are appointed by the Lord and as a result they have the gift of preaching.

THE POWER OF THE ANGELS IN HEAVEN

People who have no idea of the spiritual world and its influence into this world cannot grasp the fact that angels have real power. They think that angels have no actual substance and therefore can do nothing in effect. But those who think more deeply about such things see it very differently. They realise that all the power a person has comes from his motivation and his understanding, as without these he could not move a single muscle.

Motivation and understanding in people are governed by the Lord through the influence of spirits and angels, even down to movement and gestures. Believe it or not, a person cannot take a single step without this heavenly influence. What a spiritual person thinks, his mouth says; what he intends, his body does, even to being given strength according to his desire.

Angels have the power to cast out hundreds of thousands of evil spirits and to send them back into hell. It needs to be appreciated, though, that angels do not have any power of their own, because all their strength comes to them from the Lord.

In fact, they themselves are only powerful as far as they recognise this. Anyone who believes in his own strength promptly becomes so weak that he cannot resist even one evil spirit. This is the reason why angels take no credit to themselves, refusing praise and honour for what they do. They attribute it all to the Lord and give him praise and honour.

LANGUAGE AND SPEECH IN HEAVEN

Angels talk to each other in the same way that people do in the world. They discuss all sorts of things — household matters, communal life, moral matters, and spiritual life. There is scarcely any difference except that their level of talking is more intelligent than that of people, being more profound from deeper thought.

Angelic speech, like human speech, takes the form of separate words. It is spoken out loud, and the angels hear everything that is said because they have mouths, tongues and ears, just as people do. There is also an atmosphere through which their speech is carried, but it is a spiritual atmosphere which is adapted to spiritual beings, who breathe and speak by means of it.

There is one universal language in heaven and everyone understands everyone else perfectly well, no matter from which community they come, near or far away. This language does not have to be learned because it is the native tongue to all. It actually flows from their affections and thinking. The sounds of the language correspond to the affections, and the words themselves correspond to the thoughts that come from these affections. This is what makes the language spiritual; it is affection sounding and thought speaking. This is also how angels know what another person is really like simply from the way he speaks.

The angelic language has nothing in common with any human language except just a few words which derive their sounds from affections. The difference between the two can be shown in the inability of angels to utter even a single word of any human language. They have in fact tried, and they couldn't speak it because they can only pronounce sounds that agree completely with their affections.

The celestial angels talk from a deeper level of affection because they are in a greater love to the Lord. They talk from wisdom. The spiritual angels talk from intelligence because they are in love towards the neighbour. Celestial angels have speech that sounds rather like a gentle stream, soft and unbroken in its sound, while the speech of spiritual angels sounds crisp and clear.

And there is a kind of harmony in angelic speech as a whole coming from the heavenly form which makes the pattern for all communication there.

THE WAY IN WHICH ANGELS SPEAK WITH PEOPLE

When angels speak with people it is in the language of the person and not in their own language. The reason for this is that when angels are talking with someone, they turn towards him and join themselves to him, which brings the two into a similar kind of thinking. And as a person's thinking is linked to his memory, where speech comes from, the two of them can use the same language. When an angel or spirit makes this link with a person, he enters the whole of the person's memory, so much so that as far as he is aware he knows everything that the person knows.

The speech of angels with people sounds just as audible as that between two people, but it is only audible to the person himself, not to people nearby.

Talking with spirits, though, is rare these days because it is dangerous. This is because spirits know what the person does not know, that they are with someone. Evil spirits are by nature ones who harbour murderous feelings towards people, and they want to do nothing else than to destroy them soul and body. In fact this happens with those people who overindulge in fantasies to the point that they cut themselves off from any normal natural pleasures.

People who lead a solitary existence may hear spirits talking with them at times and there is no harm done. But the spirits who are with them are withdrawn from time to time by the Lord so that they may not know they are with the person. Most spirits are unaware that there is any other world than the one they are in, or that there are people somewhere else. So a person is not allowed to carry on a conversation with them, because, if he were to speak, the spirits would know this.

People who think all the time about religious matters and become wrapped up in them to the point of introspection, also begin to hear spirits talking with them. When religion becomes all-absorbing and an end in itself without the balance of its application to life and usefulness, it comes to preoccupy the person concerned and it takes over his whole spirit. They even enter the spiritual world and affect spirits who are there. People who are like this are visionaries who get carried away. They believe that what they hear is the Holy Spirit, when in fact there are spirits who take great delight in carrying peoples' minds away.

No-one is allowed to talk with angels except those who live by angelic standards and who recognise the Lord in his 'Divine Human'. And those who are allowed to talk can also see what is in heaven as well because they are seeing from the light of heaven in which their inner thoughts are.

WRITING IN HEAVEN

Just as angels speak by using words, they also have writing. Their minds convey ideas and meanings through writing as well as through speech. There are books in heaven which are provided by the Lord. These are primarily for the sake of the Word, which as divine truth is the very source of all heavenly wisdom, both for angels and for people. The Word itself was given by the Lord directly and it filters through the heavens in an orderly way, finally coming to rest with people. It is therefore adapted to the perception of both angels and people.

This is why the angels also have the Word which they read as people on earth do. They draw all their beliefs, teaching, and preaching from it. It is the very same Word, except that its natural sense — which is the literal meaning to us — is absent in heaven. There is a spiritual meaning instead, which is its inner meaning.

It is widely held in the world that the Word is divine down to the very last letter, but it isn't known wherein this divine quality lies. In the highest heaven, writing is formed from curved, rounded letters which are in keeping with the heavenly form. And wonderful to say, angels know this way of writing without needing to be taught, as it is given to them in the same way as the language of heaven is given. So this writing is heavenly writing. The earliest people on earth had this kind of writing before letters were invented and it carried over into the language in which the Word was originally written. This is why there are divine things in the Word and hidden meanings even in the minute forms of the original letters.

Angels can express their thoughts and affections with great precision through this writing in heavenly script. Their writing contains many hidden things which cannot be fathomed merely from thought. In the lower heavens, though, this kind of writing does not exist. There writing is very much as it is in the world with similar kinds of letters. But even so, it would be incomprehensible to people because it is in the angelic language of heaven. This writing can express in a few words more than people could describe in many written pages.

It is worth mentioning that this heavenly writing flows quite naturally from angelic thinking, effortlessly and without any hesitation. It is projected thought, and since the words themselves correspond to the thoughts of angels, they come spontaneously.

THE INNOCENCE OF ANGELS IN HEAVEN

Few people in the world know what innocence is, and no-one who is evil knows anything at all about it. It is a visible quality that can be seen on the face, in speech, and in movement, particularly in children. People do not know what it is, even less that it is where heaven itself is stored up within a person. There is, however, an innocence of childhood and an innocence of wisdom. The first kind is not real innocence, being only in an outward form, and yet it is possible to learn about true innocence from it. It glows on the faces of little children, in some of their movements, and from their earliest speech. Little children themselves do not have deeper thoughts because as yet they do not know the difference between good and evil. As a result they do not have any self-motivation or any evil intentions. They do not credit anything for themselves because they see that everything comes from their parents. They are content and happy with the little things they are given. They don't worry about food, clothing, or the future. They don't look enviously at the world. They love their parents and other people round them and allow themselves to be led by them, happily listening and obeying. This childhood innocence is the means by which they learn manners, speech, memory, and thought, and the means by which these same things are stored up in them. Yet even so, this innocence is only outward because it belongs to the body and not the mind.

The innocence of wisdom, on the other hand, is real innocence because it lies within. It comes from intentions and thoughts that are in the mind. Where there is innocence in these things, there is wisdom. This is why it is said in heaven that innocence is in wisdom, and also that an angel is wise only so far as he is in innocence. Angels then do not take credit for any good in themselves but ascribe everything they have received to the Lord. They want to be led by him.

They love what is good and they delight in the truth. They live content with what they have, whether little or much, knowing that they have as much as is good for them to have. Nor are they anxious about the future. And because all they want is to be led by the Lord and to credit him with everything they receive, they are kept safe from their own selfish tendencies, and the more they are, the more the Lord flows in. Innocence is the very essence of heaven. This is the reason why no-one can enter heaven unless he has the quality of innocence within.

THE PEACE OF ANGELS IN HEAVEN

It is hard to describe the kind of peace that the angels have in heaven. It can only be compared to that 'peace of mind' of those people who are content in God.

There are two fundamental heavenly qualities: innocence and peace, both of which come from the Lord himself. Innocence is the source of everything good in heaven, and peace is the source of all the delight of what is good. Every good has its own delight and they both come from love. Both innocence and peace, then, come from the Lord's divine love and they affect angels from their very hearts.

The source of peace is the divine peace that is in the Lord himself. It comes from the union of the Divine itself and the 'Divine Human' in him. So peace is something divine, deeply affecting everything in heaven with happiness and especially with joy. Peace is the Lord's link with heaven and with each individual there. From it as a consequence angels receive everything as a blessing and they feel what people call heavenly joy.

These qualities lie hidden away in people so long as they

are living in the world, and are only revealed when they leave their bodies and enter the spiritual world where all things are laid bare.

Since divine peace comes when what is good and what is true are united, angels are at peace when they are in a loving state, for then everything in them is united. On hearing that in the world peace is seen as the cessation of hostilities or as the removal of problems, angels say that these in themselves are not peace at all. Real peace, they say, is only with those people who are in heavenly good because only in that is peace possible. It actually flows from the Lord into the centre of such people and down to their lower levels, bringing peace in their inner mind, calm to their outer mind, and joy as a result.

THE LINK BETWEEN HEAVEN
AND THE HUMAN RACE

Many people know that everything good is from God, that nothing good is from people, and that evil is from the devil. None of this could be so unless there were a link between people and heaven, and a link with hell, and that these links were with a person's intentions and his understanding.

There are good spirits and evil spirits with each individual, through whom a person has a link with heaven and with hell. These spirits are in a world of spirits which is midway between heaven and hell and which will be described in due course.

Spirits never know that they are linked with any person; but when they are with anyone they believe that his memories and thoughts are their own. The spirits who are

61

with a person are of the same quality as his own love; but the good spirits are linked to him by the Lord whereas the person himself invites the evil ones. The spirits who are with a person, though, are changed as is life and what he loves changes. So he has some spirits with him in early childhood, others in later childhood, others in young adulthood and maturity, and still others in old age.

Innocent spirits are present in early childhood, who are themselves linked with the heaven of innocence; spirits who have a love for learning are present in later childhood; spirits who have an affection for truth and use are present in young adulthood and in maturity; and in old age, spirits are present who are involved in wisdom and innocence.

This link between angels and people only exists with those people who can be reformed in their understanding and so can be regenerated. It is different with people who can't be changed. Good spirits are certainly with them too so that they can be restrained from evil by them as far as possible, but their direct link is with evil spirits who are in communication with hell. As a result, they have the same kind of spirits with them as they themselves are as people. If they love themselves, or money, revenge, or adultery, then similar spirits who love these things are with them. These spirits almost take up residence in their evil desires. So far as the person cannot be kept from doing something evil by the good spirits, these evil spirits set him on fire. And so far as this desire rules him, they cling on and do not leave. So an evil person is linked with hell and a good person is linked with heaven.

This government of a person by the Lord by means of spirits takes place in the way that it does because a person in the world is not in the heavenly pattern. He is born with tendencies towards evil things that belong to hell and which are the very opposite of divine order. So he needs to be brought back into the heavenly pattern which is only possible by means of this indirect association with spirits. If people were born into the heavenly pattern it would be entirely different, for then they would not need to be governed by the Lord through spirits but they could be led by means of order itself which would flow in generally. In fact, a person here is governed by this general influence into such things as come from his thinking and desiring into actions, like speech and behaviour. Both of these flow in directly, so that spirits who are linked with him have nothing in common with these.

It is also important to realise that the Lord himself flows into each individual in keeping with the heavenly pattern, into a person's deepest levels as well as his more outward ones, and he arranges these to receive heaven. This influence is called a direct one, whereas the influence of spirits is indirect. The second one is made possible by means of the first.

Spirits do not introduce their own thoughts into a person but rather an affection of a love for what is good and true or for what is evil and false. As this is the case, a person has a basic choice between what is good and what is evil, and he is free in himself to choose between the two.

By thinking about it he is able to accept what is good and reject what is evil because he knows what is good and evil from reading the Word. And what he accepts becomes part of him; and what he rejects does not.

People who think more deeply about things are able to see that everything is connected to a source and that what isn't connected will disintegrate. Nothing can exist by itself; everything must come from something that was there before it. They also realise that existence is a continual coming into being. It is not easy to describe how this is so but we can broadly say that the natural world is connected to the spiritual world which is the origin of all the correspondence between them, and also that there is the same corresponding connection between everything to do with a person and everything of heaven.

Since mankind has severed this connection with heaven by turning away from heaven towards the world and himself, the Lord has provided the means of keeping the link between heaven and the human race. This intermediate link is the Word.

The Word is written in such a way that all the words in it and their meanings are correspondences, so that they have within them the spiritual or inner meaning in which angels are involved. When a person reads the Word and understands its literal meaning, the angels who are with him are understanding its inner meaning simultaneously. Angels think spiritually and people think naturally. The two seem different, but they are nevertheless one because they correspond. They make one almost like a speaker's words and their effect on a listener who is not focussing on the words as such but on their meaning.

The Word also links heaven with those people who are outside the Church. The Lord's Church is universal and is in all people who recognise something divine and who live in love to their neighbour. When these people die, they are taught by angels and they gladly accept divine truths. This universal Church is like one single person in the sight of the Lord, just as heaven is. But the Church where the Word is found and where the Lord is known by means of it is like the 'heart and lungs' within that person, by means of which all the organs and members of the body draw their life.

Angels say that if a person knew that this inner meaning existed and he did his thinking from some knowledge of it when he read the Word, he would become wiser and would be closely linked to heaven. Through this he would come into the same kind of thoughts as angels have.

BOTH HEAVEN AND HELL ARE PEOPLED FROM THE HUMAN RACE

There are no pre-created angels in heaven nor are there any devils in hell who were created as angels of light and then cast down. All those who are in heaven and hell come from the human race without any exception. This can be confirmed from the similarity between the minds of angels and those of people. Both have the ability to understand, to perceive, to reason about various things, and to intend or will; both types of mind have been formed to be able to receive heaven. The human mind is potentially just as capable of growing wise as the angel mind is, and the reason that it does not is that here in the world it is limited to the physical level in which the mind thinks naturally.

It is quite different after death, however, for then the mind no longer thinks naturally but spiritually about ideas which are unintelligible and inexpressible to a person's natural mind. It thinks and understands like an angel. This confirms that the inner part of a person — his spirit — is essentially an angel which, when released from its earthly body, is both human and angelic in potential.

When this inner part of a person, though, has not been opened towards higher things but only to lower ones, then, when it is released from the body, it is in a human form, but one which is devilish. It cannot look up to heaven but only down to hell.

Those who understand how divine order works will also perceive that a person is created to become an angel because the foundation of heavenly and angelic life can be formed in him. Divine order never stops unfinished but progresses to the final level in which it takes on its own form and multiplies. The seed-bed of heaven, then, is at this human level, in the procreation of people to become angels in heaven.

THE CASE OF PEOPLE WHO ARE BORN OUTSIDE THE CHURCH

It is generally thought that people who are born outside the church cannot be saved because they have neither the Word nor the knowledge of the Lord without which there is no salvation. Yet one fact alone shows that they are saved — truth that the Lord's mercy is universal, going out to all people individually. Those who are born outside the church are born just as human as people born in the church who are, after all, relatively few in number. It is not their fault that they have no knowledge of the Lord.

Reason tells us that no-one is born to go to hell because the Lord is actually Love itself and his love is a desire to save everyone. So he ensures that every person has some idea of religion by which they may have a sense of something divine and a deeper level to life. Living by one's religion simply means living from deeper considerations about life. Then the person is focusing on what is of the Lord. So far as this is so, a person focuses not on the world but moves his thought away from this more outward consideration of life.

We can see that everyone may be saved when we understand what makes heaven in a person. Heaven is within him and anyone who has heaven within him comes into heaven. Heaven in a person is recognising the Divine and being led by the Divine. The foremost essential in every religion is recognition of what is divine, without which there is no religion. The laws of every religion centre on worship — that is, on how the Lord is to be worshipped so that this may be acceptable to him. And when this is the desire in a person's mind, then he is being led by the Lord.

Those who are outside the church lead just as upright and moral lives as Christians do — some of them more so. A moral life is followed either for the sake of something divine or for the sake of people in the world. The two are not the same; outwardly they may look alike but inwardly they are quite different. The one saves a man, the other doesn't. The person who lives a moral life for the sake of what is divine is being led by the Lord, while the person who lives a moral life for the sake of people in the world is being led by himself.

An example may be useful to clarify this distinction. A person who does not wrong his neighbour because it is against religion is refraining from a spiritual motive. A person who refrains because he is afraid of the law, or of losing his reputation, his prestige, or his profit, in other words for his own sake, refrains from doing wrong from a natural motive and he is being led by himself. A person whose moral life is spiritual has heaven within him, but a person whose moral life is not spiritual does not have heaven within him. The reason for this is because heaven flows in from a higher level and opens a person's inner levels, flowing through these into his outward life; whereas the world flows in from a lower level and only affects the more outward levels of life and not inner ones.

The state of heaven in one person and in another varies enormously. It varies according to the quality of heavenly ideals within him. Those then, who are outside the church, while they may not be directly aware of true ideas, will ultimately accept them in the other life because of the love that they have.

While it is true that there is no salvation apart from the Lord, it should be understood that this more accurately means that there is not salvation except from the Lord.

CHILDREN IN HEAVEN

Some people have the belief that only children who are born within the church can enter heaven, and not children born outside the church. They say that children within the church have been baptised and so have been introduced into the faith of the church. But such people do not know that no-one enters heaven or gains faith merely through baptism. Baptism simply serves as a sign and a reminder that the person needs to be reborn.

It should be known that every child, wherever he was

born, is accepted by the Lord when he dies and is brought up by angels. As he grows in understanding and wisdom, he is introduced into heaven and becomes an angel.

Children who die are just as much children in the other life as they would have been here. They have the same childlike mind, the same innocence, the same gentleness. And yet they are only potentially angels at this stage, becoming angels in due course and without exception. Everyone who passes from this life finds himself in a similar state as here; the child is a child, the youth is a youth, the adult and the elderly likewise. Later, though, each person's apparent state of life does change. Children have this advantage over that of others — that they are still in innocence and evil has not yet been grounded in them by their life. Their innocence is such that all the heavenly qualities can be implanted in them because innocence is the receptacle of heaven.

The state of children in the other life is much better than that of children here, because they are not clothed with a physical body with all its restrictions, but with one like an angel's. Little children here have to learn how to walk, how to co-ordinate their movements, and how to talk. Even their senses have to develop gradually by practice. The physical body is in itself solid; it receives its sensations not from within but from outside. It is different with little children in the other life. Being spirit, they act spontaneously in accord with what is within them, walking without practice, even talking, although at first without a sequence of ideas. Yet even this ability soon develops because their outward form is at one with their inner state.

As soon as children are resuscitated, which happens

immediately after they die, they are taken into heaven and given into the care of certain angel women who, during their earth life, had loved babies and had also loved God. Because of this special quality, these women accept the children as their own. And the children, from their inborn nature, love these women as though they were their own mothers. Each woman looks after as many children as she wants, according to her spiritual parental love.

Children in heaven are right on the line along which angels look toward the Lord. They are in the region of heaven which is directly under the Lord's sight and care.

Let us now describe how children are brought up in heaven. They learn to talk from their guardians, and to begin with their speech is simply the sounds of their affections which gradually become clearer as ideas begin to develop. All angelic speech is composed of thought-forms that spring from affection.

First of all, lovely things that surround them are gently instilled into their affections and given them to see. Because these objects are spiritual in origin, heavenly things flow in at the same time that the children see them. In this way, the children's inner levels are opened, so that, day by day, they become more perfect. When this first stage is established, the children are taken to another part of heaven where they are taught, and so the process continues. They are taught mainly by means of representations of things which are suitable for their particular level of understanding — representations so beautiful to see and so full of wisdom that they defy description.

When the children have acquired wisdom and understanding, they become angels, not now looking like children any longer, but like adults, with an adult wisdom and perception. And the reason that child-angels come to look more mature as they grow in wisdom is because wisdom is spiritual nourishment. The very things that feed their minds also feed their bodies. This is from correspondence, for the form of their bodies is nothing but the outward expression of their life within.

It is worth knowing further that children in heaven do not appear to age beyond the onset of young adulthood, and they stay like that for ever.

THE WISE AND THE SIMPLE IN HEAVEN

It is widely held that intelligence is a matter of scholarship and learning, and that therefore the wise will have more glory and distinction in heaven than the simple. Yet heavenly intelligence is not of this nature. It is an inner intelligence which comes from a love of what is true, not for the sake of worldly or heavenly glory but for the sake of the truth itself, which fills the angels with deep emotion and delight. People who are moved and delighted by what is true are being affected by the light of heaven, and if they are moved by this, then they are moved by divine truth and in fact by the Lord himself. This is because the light of heaven is the Lord in heaven.

The light of heaven can only enter and affect the deeper levels of the mind since these have been specially formed to receive this light. It enters in such a way that it affects the mind and fills it with delight, for anything that flows in from heaven and is received has within itself something delightful and pleasant. This is the origin of genuine affection for what is true. People who have this affection and receive the truth are said to shine in heaven. But those who seek truth for their own glory cannot shine in heaven because they are only in worldly light, which in itself is darkness. Indeed, self-glory is their chief motive and the only end in view. When this is the case, the person in question focuses on himself first and simply uses truth as a means to an end. As a result he turns his sight away from heaven to the world, and away from the Lord to himself. Outwardly, this sort of person may seem to be just as erudite or learned as those who are truly in the light of heaven. This is because they speak in the same way; sometimes, outwardly, they seem to be even wiser because they are prompted by self-glory and have become skilled in the imitation of heaven. Yet all the while they are completely different within, and this difference is clearly seen by the angels.

The qualities that a person acquires or develops here in the world stay with him; he takes them with him when he dies. They continue to develop after death, but only to the extent of his affection for what is true and his desire to put that to good use. Those with little desire develop little; those with much desire develop greatly. Yet each receives as much as he is capable of receiving, for love draws everything that agrees with it to itself. This is what the Lord said, that *"to everyone that has, it shall be given, so that he shall have a greater abundance."* (Matthew 13:12).

True intelligence and wisdom lie in perceiving what is good and true, and consequently in seeing what is evil and false for what it is, and so clearly distinguishing between the two from an inner perception. To become intelligent and wise, a person needs to keep learning many things, not only the things of heaven and of spiritual life, but also the ways of the world. So far as a person keeps learning and applies what he has learned to life, he becomes intelligent and wise, because he is being perfected.

Simple people of this sort are those whose inner levels are opened but are not developed by means of spiritual or natural truths. They perceive that things are true when they hear them but they do not see them in themselves. Wise people of this sort are those whose inner levels are not only opened but are developed as well. They both see truths within themselves and perceive them.

THE RICH AND THE POOR IN HEAVEN

People have all kinds of ideas about who is accepted into heaven. Some imagine that the poor may enter, but not the rich; some believe that rich and poor alike are received; while others believe that the rich cannot enter heaven until they have given up their wealth and become poor. These opinions are often based on passages from the Bible.

But people who distinguish between rich and poor concerning their entrance into heaven fail to understand the meaning of the Bible, which is talking about spiritual matters even though it is expressed in natural images.

Literalists, then, may well miss the point of such passages where it is said for example that *"it is as hard for the rich to enter heaven as for a camel to go through the eye of a needle"* or that *"blessed are the poor, for theirs is the kingdom of heaven"*. Those who understand the Bible spiritually see the meaning otherwise. They know that heaven is for all people whose lives are based on faith and love, regardless of whether they are rich or poor. No-one is denied heaven on account of his wealth, nor received into heaven on account of his poverty. Both rich and poor are in heaven, and many of the rich are in greater glory and happiness there than the poor. It needs to be understood precisely who are meant by the 'rich' and the 'poor' in the Bible.

A man may live outwardly as a man of the world, becoming rich, enjoying the good things of life, and none of this will be an obstacle to his entering heaven, provided that in himself he thinks about God in the way that he should, and provided that he treats his neighbour fairly.

A person's actions, by which he is said to be judged in the Word, are really his thoughts and his affections which prompt what he does. It can be seen then that a person's outward way of life achieves nothing in respect of his salvation, but only the condition of his inner life. The actions of two people may be identical, but within they may be completely different.

Since one person can live outwardly like another in every way, provided that within himself he thinks about God and wishes well to his neighbour, it can be seen that it is not so difficult as many people believe to proceed along the way to heaven. The only difficulty is being able to resist the love of self and of the world, and to stop this from predominating, because this is the cause of every evil. So far as a person resists the evils that come from self-love and worldly desires, he is being led by the Lord and not by himself. Then the Lord resists these things within the person and is able to remove them.

74

It is a life of love and use — doing what is just and right in each situation — that leads to heaven; it is not a life of piety or renunciation of the world. For only when a person is involved in normal activities can his life find expression and begin to grow in training for heaven. If he withdraws from involvement in the world, this development cannot happen. Each individual's life remains with him after death, whether he be rich or poor. There is no special admission for one more than for another. The person who has lived well comes into heaven and the person who has lived in evil does not.

Riches can be made to serve great use in the world and a rich person may provide more benefits than a poor person can. If riches are used in this way, they also serve to withdraw the mind of the person from idleness, which is destructive because in it a person thinks evilly from the evil that is natural to him. But it is entirely different with riches that are loved as an end in themselves. After death these become squalid and decay like a body without a soul.

Poor people do not enter heaven because of their poverty, but because of their life. Poverty itself is able to lead a person away from heaven, just as much as wealth can. Many poor people become discontented, or envious, or believe that riches are blessings, and when they do not get them they are provoked, especially against providence. But it is a very different matter with poor people who are content with their lot, who are reliable and hardworking, preferring work to idleness, and who live carefully and well.

Confusion about the lot of the 'rich' and the 'poor' after death often comes from a misunderstanding of the Bible, where both are mentioned frequently. There the 'rich' generally stand for those people who possess much spiritual knowledge of what is good and true — that is, those who are within the church, where the Word is. The 'poor' stand for those who lack this knowledge but who nevertheless long for it.

MARRIAGES IN HEAVEN

Since heaven is formed from the human race, and since there are angels of both sexes in heaven, and since woman is for man and man is for woman, it follows that there are marriage relationships in heaven, just as there are here in the world. Marriage, in the way that it exists in heaven, is the growing together of two individual people into one mind. This union needs to be explained. The human mind itself is made up of two parts, one of which is called 'understanding' and the other 'will'. When these two are working in conjunction they make a single mind. In heaven the husband takes the part of 'understanding' and the wife that of 'will'. When this union, which is an inner bond between them, finds expression outwardly and physically, it is felt as love. This love is true marriage love, which comes from the union of two individuals into one mind. In heaven, this is called 'living together' and the two are spoken of as one, even as being one angel. This union comes from the form in which man and woman are created. Man is born to be discerning and to reflect from his understanding, whereas woman is born to be affectionate, to reflect from her will. This can be seen, both in their own dispositions, and in their physical form and its appearance. A man has a more rugged appearance, a deeper voice, and a firmer body; a woman is softer in her features, with a gentler voice and a greater beauty. The same difference is true of the understanding and the will.

This is why the spiritual meaning of references to 'young men' and to 'virgins', or 'men' and 'women', in the Bible has to do with particular qualities of understanding and will, or affection.

Men and women each have the two faculties of understanding and affection, but in the man it is his understanding that leads, while in a woman it is her will, and the character of the person comes from what is uppermost in him. And yet there is no sense of dominance in heavenly marriages. The wife's intention actually belongs to her husband, and his understanding similarly belongs to his wife, because each one wants to share the purpose and the thoughts of the other one. This is how they are made one. This union is an actual union in the full sense because the wife's will enters her husband's understanding, and his understanding enters her will, and this happens especially when they are looking into each other's faces. There is a full and open sharing of thoughts and feelings in heaven, and all the more so between a husband and wife there, because they love each other.

The source of true marriage love is the union of truth and good which are from the Lord; this is why the union of good and truth in heaven is called the 'heavenly marriage'. So far as the truth within a person is united to what is good in him, he is joined to the Lord and heaven. Marriage love is the greatest expression of this. In the coming together of minds in marriage — and in the love that results — there is the desire that what is one's own be the other's, and this desire is mutual. It is the same in marriage as within the individual person — when a person thinks what he wills, and wills what he thinks, he is then of one mind.

THE WORK THAT ANGELS DO IN HEAVEN

The jobs that are done by angels are too many and varied to be described in detail and they can only be dealt with generally. Each community in heaven has its own particular work to do, for just as communities are distinguished by their qualities of good, they are also distinguished by the use they provide, as good is shown through action, which is use. Everyone in heaven is actively useful because the Lord's kingdom is a kingdom of uses.

From everything that has been said so far about heaven — its worship, its government, its houses and homes, and its marriages — it is clear that there are many different occupations and responsibilities in heaven and within each community there.

Everything in heaven is organised according to the divine pattern, which is maintained through the responsibilities that are undertaken by angels. Matters of common good are the concern of the wiser angels, while more specific uses are dealt with by angels who are less wise, and so on. These uses are seen according to the exact way in which they form part of the divine design. The value of each occupation is seen in the use that it serves, and yet the angels do not claim the worth of what they do, but rather attribute it all to the use itself. And as the use is in the good that is done, and all good is from the Lord, they attribute everything they do to him.

From this principle, one can see the nature of the hierarchy of angels in heaven. The extent to which a particular use in heaven is loved and valued will determine the love and respect that is shown to the person who performs that particular use.

This respect is also shown in proportion to the way the person concerned attributes the use he does to the Lord and not to himself. In heaven, respect for others is on the basis of use, and not of the person. Regard for others is also from the same principle. One person is seen to be like every other, whether he is of great or small importance, the only difference being in his wisdom. And what is wisdom? It is loving what is useful, that is, the welfare of one's fellows, the community, and the Church.

There are communities whose work involves looking after babies. Other communities teach and train children as they grow up. There are others who instruct good, simple people from Christian backgrounds and lead them towards heaven. There are those who do the same for people from non-Christian backgrounds. Other communities protect newly arrived spirits from the attacks of evil spirits. There are some whose work lies in helping those people who are caught up in the 'lower earth' stage, and also others who help people in the hells, restraining them so that they cannot torment each other beyond certain bounds. And then there are the communities who help people who are being revived after death.

There are also angels who are sent to help people on earth, watching over them, leading them away from evil thoughts and feelings, and instilling what is good, so far as the people will accept this freely. When angels are with people on earth, they live, as it were, in their affections and feelings, and are near them or far from them according to the nature of the person's quality of life at the time. All these occupations are common activities among the angels, yet each individual angel has his own particular contribution, which makes part of the common use and of the divine design.

HEAVENLY JOY AND HAPPINESS

Heavenly joy comes from the delight of sharing one's own happiness and blessings with othes. And since everyone in heaven feels like that, it can be seen how much joy there is in heaven.

This sense of sharing with others which pervades the whole of heaven comes from the two underlying supreme loves in heaven which are love to the Lord and love towards the neighbour. The urge to give is inherent in both these loves. The Lord's love is the love of giving everything of itself to all others, because it seeks universal happiness. The same love exists in those who love him, because the Lord is then in them.

But love of oneself distorts this delight and diverts it from others, channelling it only towards self as its sole consideration. Love of worldly things brings the urge to covet what belongs to others. These two loves inherently work to destroy delight and happiness in other people. And if any sharing does take place, it is only done for selfish reasons.

The person who, while he lives in the world, loves himself or loves the world above all else, feels those loves to be full of delight and intensely pleasurable while he lives in the world. Yet the person who loves the Lord and his neighbour does not feel the full delight of these loves while he lives in the world, but feels only an imperceptible sense of their blessings because they lie deeply within him and are covered over by the concerns of everyday life.

All this changes after death, for then the pleasures of self-love and worldly love become filled with anguish and pain. This is because these are the nature of such loves. After death they are turned into what is called 'hell-fire'. Or at times they are turned into something filthy and disgusting according to correspondence. And strange to say these are felt to be delightful by those concerned.

But that hidden delight which was imperceptible here is changed after death into the fullest delight of heaven, perceived and felt in every possible way. This is due to its being a spiritual delight, and life in heaven is life in the spirit. Heavenly joy and happiness can also be shown by comparison with the physical senses in people. Each sense brings a feeling of delight which is in keeping with the use it provides. Sight brings pleasure from seeing beautiful things, colours and shapes; hearing brings pleasure from sweet sounds and harmonies; smell brings delight from scents and fragrance; taste from flavours; and so on. The reason that sight brings delight comes from the use that sight serves to the understanding, which is an inner sight. The reason that hearing brings delight is from the use that hearing serves for both the understanding and the will by its special sensitivity. And so with the other physical senses. The sense of touch, however, which is the purest and most exquisite expression of marriage love, is the most valuable sense of all because of its use which is the increase of the human race and therefore the number of those in heaven.

All these delights fill the senses because heaven itself flows into them. Every angel in heaven progresses continually towards the springtime of life. The more thousands of years lived, the greater and fuller is the advance, and this continues for ever. The progress is always according to the growth of love, goodness, and faith in the person concerned.

Women who die old and weary, but who have lived in the ways of heaven during their lives, come more and more into the bloom of their young womanhood as time passes, and into such beauty as has never been seen in the world. It is their inner qualities that produce this beauty and which become their outward appearance, radiating in every detail of their face. Such women are forms of love itself. In a word, to grow old in heaven is to grow young.

THE UNLIMITED SIZE OF HEAVEN

The truth that heaven is of unlimited size and extent can be clearly seen from many things that have so far been said about it. It can be seen from the fact that heaven is peopled from the human race, not only from those who are born within the church but also from those outside it who lived by what is good during their lives in the world. It can also be seen from the enormous numbers of people who at present live in the world, several thousands of whom die each day, and millions in the course of a year. This has continued since the beginning of human life over many thousands of years. All these people entered the other world when they died, and they still do so today. Most of those who lived in the earliest times became angels in heaven because then people thought more inwardly and spiritually.

The size of heaven can also be seen from the fact that all children become angels and the number of these amounts to a quarter or a fifth of the whole human race on earth. It can further be seen from the fact that every planet visible to the eye in our solar system is an earth, and beyond these are countless more earths in the universe, all full of inhabitants. In the whole universe is the Lord alone who is recognised as God of heaven and earth.

Since heaven as a whole resembles a single person and corresponds to everything in a person, it can be seen that this correspondence cannot possibly be filled up because the correspondence is not only with individual organs and tissues of the body but with every smallest part, even to ducts and fibres. There is also a correspondence with the more inward levels in a person — those things that go to make up his personality, which again are beyond number.

The reason this correspondence cannot possibly be filled is because the greater the number of communities that correspond to a specific part of the body, the more perfect heaven becomes, and this is so to infinity.

I was shown the extent of both the inhabited and the uninhabited parts of heaven and I saw that the extent of the uninhabited part of heaven was so great that it could not ever be filled, not even if there were as many people on every planet in the universe as there are on ours.

Some people believe that heaven is of small size and limited to those people of certain types — the 'elect', or the 'poor', or those for whom the Lord intercedes. But heaven is in no way closed, nor can it ever be full up. The Lord leads every individual who accepts him and who lives by the laws of the divine design which are the rules of love and faith. Every single person is born for heaven and accepted if he receives heaven into himself in the world, and shut out if he does not receive it.

DEATH AND AFTER

THE WORLD OF SPIRITS

There is a place — or state — into which every person comes after death. It is called the world of spirits and it is neither heaven nor hell but a place or state midway between the two. When a person dies, he comes first into the world of spirits, and then, after some time there, he is either raised up into heaven or drawn down into hell, depending on the quality of his life in the world.

The world of spirits, being a midway place between heaven and hell, is also a midway state of the person after his death. Hell is below and heaven above. So long as a person is in the world of spirits, he is not yet in either heaven or hell.

For heaven in a person is the uniting together of what is good and what is true in him, and hell is the uniting of what is evil with what is false in him. Whenever what is good has been fully integrated with what is true in a person who is a spirit, he comes into heaven, and whenever evil and false things are fully integrated in a person, he comes into hell.

It is the process of unification that takes place in the world of spirits, because a person is then in a midway state. So long as a person has a separate understanding and intention he will remain in this midway state. Most people

85

are like this, having some knowledge of what is true and yet giving only some, little or no thought to this.

In order, then, for a person to be in heaven or in hell, he is brought first into the world of spirits when he dies so that this final harmony of those things that are within him may be achieved. For no-one in heaven or in hell is allowed to continue to have a divided mind, that is, to think one way and intend another, but everyone must fully understand what his intentions are and intend to do what he understands.

In heaven, a person who desires to do what is good will also understand what is true, while in hell, those who intend to do evil will understand everything that is false. So in the world of spirits false notions and ideas are removed from those people who are basically good and replaced with true ideas that are in harmony with their good. True ideas, on the other hand, are removed from evil people and replaced with false ideas that match their evil intentions.

There are vast numbers of people in the world of spirits because this is where everyone first gathers together. This is also where everyone is closely scrutinised and made ready for heaven or for hell. The length of time spent in the world of spirits is not fixed. Some people simply enter and then are almost immediately taken to either heaven or hell; some stay for a few weeks, some for several years, but not more than thirty. The period of time depends on the correspondence — or the lack of it — between the person's more inward and outward levels of life.

Immediately a person enters the world of spirits, the Lord provides that he is linked with a community which has the same love that led the person while he was in the world. The evil person is immediately linked with one of the communities in hell and the good person is similarly linked with one of the heavenly communities. Yet even though they are distinguished like this, newcomers to the world of spirits are able to mix freely with whomever they wish to meet. Friends, relations, husbands and wives, can meet and talk whenever they wish. I saw one father with his six sons, each of whom he recognised, but because they were of very different natures as a result of their life in the world, they soon separated. People who move on from the world of spirits into heaven or hell, however, no longer see or know each other unless they have a similar disposition that comes from the love each of them has. They see each other in the world of spirits because there, people are passing through one state after another just as they did during their life in the world; but afterwards, every person is brought into a permanent state that is fixed by the love that leads them most, and in this state people recognise one another only by being in similar loves. For what is alike joins and what is unlike separates.

Since the world of spirits is a midway state between heaven and hell with each individual, so it is also a midway place with hell below and heaven above it. All the communities of hell are closed off from the world of spirits and are only open to it through holes and cracks like those in rocks and also through wider openings which are so well guarded that no-one can come out unless permitted, which they are on occasion for special reasons. Heaven, also, is closed on every side from the world of spirits, and there is no entrance open to any community in heaven except by a narrow way, the entrance to which is also well guarded.

The world of spirits looks like a valley that is among mountains and cliffs. It is higher or lower here and there. The entrances to the heavenly communities are invisible to everyone except to those who are ready for heaven. There is one single entrance out of the world of spirits to each heavenly community which leads along a single path that then branches into several paths as it climbs.

The entrances to the communities of hell are also invisible save to those who are about to enter, to whom they are opened. When open, one can see dark, sooty-looking caves which lead down a slope into the depths where again there are many gates. Disgusting smells drift out from those caves, which good spirits flee from because they are revolted by them, whereas evil spirits greedily follow these smells because they find them delightful. Just as each evil spirit found pleasure in his own brand of evil while he was in the world, so after death he is then delighted with the particular stench to which his evil corresponds. I once heard a person in the world of spirits screaming in torment when a breath of heaven reached him, yet he was calm and happy while a breath of hell was reaching him.

Each person also has two entrances within him — one that opens towards hell and the evil and false influences that come from there, and the other that opens towards heaven and the good and true influences that come from there. The gate of hell is open in people who are involved in something evil and so also in false ideas. Light from heaven can only enter through chinks overhead, enabling such people to think, to use logic and to talk. On the other hand, the gate of heaven is open in people who are involved in what is good and so also in true ideas. For there are two ways which lead to a person's rational mind

— a higher or inward way, by which things that are good and true flow in from the Lord; and a lower or outward way, by which things that are evil and false can climb in from hell. A person's rational mind is the centre towards which both these ways lead, and therefore a person is rational in proportion to the amount of heavenly light that he lets into his mind.

So far as this light is not let in, his rationality fades, even though the person may seem to be rational to himself.

All of this is mentioned here to show the correspondence of a person with heaven and hell. As the rational mind is being formed it corresponds to the world of spirits, the things above it to heaven, and the things below it to hell. Those who are ready for heaven have their rational mind opened upwards and closed below, while those who are ready for hell have their rational mind opened downwards and closed above. These, then, can only look downwards towards hell, whereas the others can only look upwards towards heaven.

Looking up means looking to the Lord since he is the centre to which all heaven looks. Looking down means turning away from the Lord towards an opposite centre on which hell focuses. The whole of hell faces away from the Lord.

EVERY PERSON IS A SPIRIT

The immortal soul of a person is his spirit which is the part of him that thinks and lives. The body is really only a kind of accessory to the spirit by which a person can lead a useful life in a natural, material world. The spirit is the actual person himself and this is why, when a person's body is separated from his spirit, which is called dying, he is still a person and is alive. I have heard from heaven that some who die are thinking even while they lie on the slab in their cold body before they are resuscitated. As far as they themselves know, they are still alive, except that they are unable to move the smallest part of their body.

Since the spirit is the person himself it follows that the spirit of a person is in just as definite a form as his body is, that is, in a human form, and that it enjoys sensations just as much when it is separated from the physical body as when it was within it. This can be seen from the fact that a person cannot think or will anything without the means of doing so — a subject or a substance from which things proceed and in which things occur. There is no reality to anything which is thought to exist without a substance. There is no sight without an organ of sight, and no hearing without an organ to hear with. The same is true of thought; unless this happens in and from a substance — an organic form — it could not happen at all.

This is why spirits, just like people, see, hear and feel after they are released from the body; not now in a natural world but in the spiritual world. The natural senses that the spirit had while it was within the body came from the material part that was added to it then; but even then it felt and sensed spiritually in thinking and willing.

Two situations can be added here to show that a person as to his inner levels is a spirit and that this spirit is in the form of a substantial body.

Every person, while living in the body, is in a community of spirits as far as his own spirit is concerned, even though he is unaware of this fact. A good person is in an angelic community and an evil person is in a hellish community, and each person enters that same community after he dies. Yet the person is not visible in that community while he lives in the world because he is then thinking on a natural level. But when people think in a manner that is withdrawn from the body and are in the spirit, they sometimes appear in their own community. And when they are seen they are easily distinguished from the spirits who are there because they go about in silent meditation and thought, not looking at anyone else and apparently not seeing them. As soon as any spirit speaks to them they disappear.

The other instance is that of being withdrawn from the body. It is like this. A person is brought into a state which is midway between sleep and wakefulness, and when he is in that state he seems to himself to be wide awake. Every sense is alert as when he is fully awake — sight and hearing — and the sense of touch is then more acute than ever it is during normal body wakefulness. In this state, angels and spirits have been seen clearly, and heard, and even touched. In this state almost nothing of the physical body intervenes. This is the state that is called 'being out of the body and not knowing whether one is in the body or out of it'.

HOW A PERSON WAKES AFTER DEATH AND ENTERS ETERNAL LIFE

Once the physical body can no longer function in the natural world, the person dies. This happens when the motion of the lungs and the heart stops. Yet the person does not die. He is simply separated from the body which served him in the world. The person himself still lives on because he is spirit. He simply crosses over from one world into another. When 'death' is mentioned in the Bible, it actually refers in its inner meaning to resurrection and the continuation of life.

There is a deep communication of the spirit with the breathing and the beating of the heart — thought with breathing and feeling with the heartbeat. So when these two motions stop working in the body, there is an immediate separation of the spirit. They are the actual bonds whose breaking leaves the spirit to itself, and the body, now deprived of the life of its spirit, grows cold and begins to decay.

After the separation, the person's spirit continues to be in his body for a while, but only until the heart has finally stopped beating. This varies according to the illness that caused death. The moment the heart stops, the person is awakened, but this is done by the Lord alone. Awakening here means drawing the spirit out of the body and into the spiritual world. This is usually called 'resurrection'.

I myself was given the experience of this awakening which enables me now to describe how it happens.

I was brought into an unconscious state so far as my physical senses were concerned, and I was virtually like a person who was dying. Yet all my inner senses remained unimpaired so that I was able to see and remember everything that happened to me — things which happen to people when they are awakened after death.

I noticed that my breathing was almost non-existent but that the more inward breathing of the spirit continued, which was connected with a slight and still breathing of the body. After this, a communication was formed between my heartbeat and the celestial kingdom, because that kingdom corresponds to the heart. I saw angels from this kingdom who were with me; some were at a distance and were sitting at my head. This led to the removal of all my own feelings of affection and yet my thought and perception continued. I was like this for some hours.

Then the spirits who were around me left, saying that I was dead. There was a slight fragrance, rather like that of an embalmed body. When celestial angels are present, all the things to do with the corpse are perceived as something fragrant, which stops spirits from approaching when they perceive it. This is how evil spirits are kept away from a person's spirit when he is just being awakened.

The angels who were by my head were silent, with only their thoughts in communication with my thoughts. When these thoughts are received by the dying person, then the angels know that the person's spirit is now in a state where it can be led out of the body. While their thoughts were being communicated, the angels looked at my face, which is the way in which thought communication takes place in heaven.

I also sensed that the angels tried to discover what I was thinking and to see whether it was like the thinking of people who die, which is normally about eternal life. I sensed they wanted to keep my mind in this way of thinking. Afterwards, I was told that a person's spirit is maintained in its last thought when the body dies, until it returns to the kind of thoughts that come from the love that led him most strongly while he was in the world.

Specifically, I was allowed to feel that there was a pulling or drawing out of what was within my mind — and so in my spirit — and that this was being drawn out from my body. I was told that this is done by the Lord and that it is the actual source of resurrection.

Celestial angels are always present when a person is being awakened. They do not leave the person because they love everyone. But when the spirit is such that he can no longer bear to be with these loving angels, he wishes to leave them. When this happens, angels from the spiritual kingdom come near who give light to the person. For up to this point he was unable to see but only to think. When this change happens, the person has the feeling that a layer is being rolled back from the left eye towards the nose, so that the eye opens and can see. It seems to the person that this is actually happening to him. When this is done, something bright but hazy can be seen, rather like images seen by a person through half-closed eyelids when he first wakes up. It was after this that I felt something being gently rolled off my face which led to a more spiritual way of thinking. This rolling served to show that the person has come from natural thinking into spiritual and the angels take the greatest care to prevent any thought springing up in the person's mind unless it savours of love. They now tell the person that he is a spirit.

Now that the person can see, the spiritual angels give every help they can to the newly-awakened person — telling him about the spiritual world and the things that are there, but only as far as he can understand this. If he has no desire to be told, the person will long to get away from the presence of these angels. But it is not the angels who move away; rather the person separates himself from them. For all angels only love; and in this particular instance, these angels love to offer help and guidance in teaching and in leading newly-awakened spirits to heaven.

When a person has then moved away from these angels, he is received by good spirits who do everything they possibly can for him as long as he is with them. But if his life in the world was of a kind that would make friendship with good spirits impossible, he then longs to get away from them as well. This pattern happens for as long and as often as is necessary, until the person comes into the presence of spirits who match the kind of life he led in the world and with whom he finds his own way of life. And then, surprisingly, he leads the same kind of life that he led while he was in the world.

This introductory phase only lasts a few days. Later, the person is led from one state into another in order to reveal the true nature of his spirit, and finally he goes into heaven or hell. All this will be described in due course. Some people are completely nonplussed by the discovery that they are alive after death. This happens particularly to those who had no belief in any life of the soul after death while they were in the world. People who are like this make friends after death with others who think the same as they do and they are separated from people who do believe. Generally speaking, these people are linked with some hellish community because, often, they have denied divine things and despised what the church teaches.

PEOPLE ARE IN A PERFECT FORM AFTER DEATH

Every spirit is in a human form, or, to put it another way, each spirit appears as a person. This is because a person is a person because of his spirit, and not because of his body, as has already been said so often.

When a person first enters the world of spirits after death, his face and voice are similar to those he had while he was in the world. The reason for this is that he is still in a more external state of life, his more inward levels being not yet opened up. This state is the first one that people have after they die. Later on, the face begins to change and becomes quite different. It takes on the appearance that comes from the love that led him most of all while he was in the world and which preoccupied his spirit while it was in his body. This love is the real person. The face of a person's spirit is very different from the face of his body. His physical face comes from his parents, while his spiritual face comes from what he loves, and is in this image. As outward features begin to fade after death, which happens when a person's inner life is opened up, the spirit increasingly comes to resemble outwardly what he loves within. I have seen people just arrived from the world, and I recognised them by their faces and voices. But when I saw them later, I did not recognise them.

Another reason why faces change is that in the other life people are not allowed to feign affections that they do not have. They are not allowed to be hypocritical. It takes much longer for the faces of hypocrites to change than others because they have practised making their life look like a copy of good affections, so much so that they appear good. As a result they seem attractive for a while. But their ability to keep up this pretence is gradually taken away from them, and the inner levels of their mind take on the form of what they love, and later on, they become even more mis-shapen than any other people.

The more inwardly a person has loved divine things and lived by them during his life, the more beautiful he becomes after death. This is because everyone's inner levels of life are opened and formed according to the quality of their love and their life. As a result, the more inward the affection, the more it shares in the form of heaven, and so the more beautiful its face. In fact, everything that is good and true that comes from the Lord and which makes heaven is in a human form. This is so, not only in a general way, but also in every smallest part and least detail. This form causes everyone in heaven to be in a human form and one which mirrors the way the Lord is received.

EVERY SENSE, MEMORY, THOUGHT, AND AFFECTION EXISTS AFTER DEATH

When a person dies, he carries everything of himself with him into the spiritual world, except his physical body. For then he has a spiritual body which seems to be no different from his natural body, except that it is made up from spiritual substances rather than natural elements. Furthermore, when something spiritual touches and sees something spiritual, it is just the same as when something natural touches and sees something natural. So, when a person has become a spirit, he cannot tell that he is not in the body that he had in the world, and so he does not know that he has died.

People who are spirits have every sense that they had while they were in the world. They see, they hear, they speak, they can smell and taste; they can even feel the pressure of being touched. In addition, such a person also continues to have longings, thoughts, reflections, affections and feelings, loves, strivings and intentions just as he had before. A person who enjoyed scholarship and study can read and write as before. In a word, when a person crosses from one life to another, it is just as if he had gone from one place to another and taken with him all the things he could do in his own right.

He even takes his memory of worldly things with him — all the things he saw, heard, read, learned, or thought from his earliest infancy right up to the last moment of his life. But because these wordly things in his memory cannot be reproduced in a spiritual environment, they become, as it were, at rest, just as they do in a person in the world when he is not thinking about them. But they can be brought back again to mind when the Lord wishes this to happen.

People whose lives are ruled purely by their physical senses are quite incapable of believing that a person's life after death is like this, because they cannot understand how it can be so. They can only think in terms of nature, even when they are thinking about spiritual things. What cannot be sensed and touched with the hands, for them, cannot possibly exist.

Yet spiritual senses as they are in the spiritual world are far more delicate and acute than the senses of this world. Those in heaven see and hear more clearly and think more wisely than when they were in this world, because now they see by the light of heaven and they hear through a spiritual atmosphere which surpasses that of the world by many degrees. The difference is like the difference between something that is crystal clear and something that is covered by cloud. Divine truth is the light of heaven and it gives the angels the ability to see the most minute detail. In addition to this, the sight of angels is in complete harmony with their understanding. Their hearing and perception act as one, giving them the ability to know a speaker's affection and thought just from the sound of his voice.

Those in the hells, on the other hand, have senses that are as imperfect with them as the senses of the angels are perfect. And every evil spirit is able to be shown his evil actions because they can be drawn out from his memory. Adultery, theft, bribery and corruption are all brought into the open, even to the very details of what happened; so much so, that there is no possibility of any denial. All this is in keeping with what the Lord himself said, that *"nothing is concealed that will not be uncovered, and nothing hidden that will not be recognised. What you have said in darkness will be heard in the light, and what you have said in the ear will be proclaimed on the housetops." (Luke 12:2-3)*

When a person's actions are being shown to him after death, the angels who have the responsibility for drawing out this information look carefully at his face. This examination then spreads all through his whole body until the whole is seen in clear light. It happens like this because the things of the memory are not only written on the brain but on the whole person. And what a person has thought, wished to do, said, or done, cannot be destroyed because they are written on his spirit.

Even though a person's worldly memory is carried into the spiritual world, the natural elements themselves are not brought out again in the other life. In their place, spiritual objects are seen that are connected to the natural ones by their correspondence. When these are seen they appear to have the same form as the natural elements. The reason for this is that every visible thing in the spiritual world looks like something natural, even though it is in itself spiritual.

If a person has only developed his mind in terms of data and factual knowledges, then when he comes into the spiritual world, where everyone speaks from their affections rather than from external knowledge, these people appear to be either simple or stupid. What they had amassed can no longer be presented because it belongs only to the world. This is why a person is rational after death to the extent that he has *developed his mind* by means of language and data in the world, and not to the extent that he was highly skilled in languages and data.

AFTER DEATH A PERSON'S QUALITY IS THE SAME AS WAS THE QUALITY OF HIS LIFE IN THE WORLD

In the Bible it is often said that a person will be judged and rewarded according to his actions during his life. Anyone who thinks in a true way cannot help but see that a person who lives well will go to heaven and that a person who lives wickedly will go to hell. Yet of course the evil person is unwilling to believe that his situation after death depends on his life in the world. He thinks that heaven is granted out of pure mercy and depends on a faith which he separates from life.

It must be seen that the character of a person is contained within his actions, and that his inner attitudes are not made real unless they are matched by what he does. These actions are the person's outward life and the quality of his inner life is expressed through them. Yet actions do not mean only the way they are presented outwardly; they also mean the way they are within the person. Everyone realises that every action springs from a person's intentions and thinking. Unless it came from this source, it would just be movement, such as machines and models might produce. So, an action is a result that comes from an inner cause.

This allows us to see what is meant by the life into which a person comes after death. It is a life that is based on his love, not only in potential, but in action as well. It is what he does, because this contains within it all the elements of what he loves and what he believes.

Each person has what is called a 'ruling love' — a love that predominates — which he keeps after death and which never changes to eternity. Every person has a number of different loves but they all trace back to his ruling love and make one with it, or taken together, compose it. Some of these loves are more outward in their nature, others are more inward; some are nearer while some are further away. But together they make up a kind of kingdom within the person and are arranged in a definite order even though the person is unaware of this. But to some degree this is made known to people in the other life, for the way in which a person extends his sphere of life around him depends on this organisation within him.

After death a person is what he loves. Death itself brings about the removal of everything that is not in harmony with a person's ruling love. If the person, then, is basically good, any parts of his character which do not fit in with this quality are removed or, as it were, carried away. In this way he is put into his own love. The same happens with an evil person, but in his case it is the true ideas that he knows which are removed or carried away. Finally each person becomes his own love, and once this has happened, the person constantly turns his face towards his love, keeping it always before his eyes whatever direction he turns to.

Every spirit can be led anywhere as long as he is kept in his ruling love. They are unable to resist even though they know what is happening and think that they will resist. Some have tried to make them act contrary to their ruling love but always to no avail. This is because their love is like a chain or rope round them by which they can, as it were, be pulled along and from which they cannot free themselves.

Even people in the world are the same; their own love leads them and they are led by others by means of their own love. All forms of communication in the other life show the truth of this fact that a person's spirit is his ruling love. So far as anyone there is doing something or talking about something which is in keeping with someone else's love, then that person is visibly there with a cheerful, lively face. But were the conversation to be contrary to someone else's ruling love, then that person's face begins to change, to grow hazy and indistinct until in the end he would vanish as if he had never been there.

Some other points may be added to show the importance of this ruling love. A person stays the way he is for ever, as far as his ruling love is concerned. A person cannot keep the faith or belief that he has, if it does not stem from a heavenly love.

And lastly, it is love in action that lasts because this is the person's own life.

AFTER DEATH THE DELIGHTS OF A PERSON'S LIFE ARE CHANGED INTO THE THINGS THAT CORRESPOND TO THEM

All the things a person finds delightful come from his ruling love because a person only takes delight in the things he loves, particularly in what he loves above all else. Everything that brings delight traces back to, and makes up, the ruling love of a person which in heaven is overall a love for the Lord, and in hell it is a love of self.

In order to see how a person's natural pleasures are changed after death into their spiritual counterparts, a knowledge of correspondence is required. Basically this teaches that nothing natural can exist without something spiritual corresponding to it. In particular it teaches what it is that corresponds and what kind of thing it is. So, anyone with this awareness can know what his own state after death will be like if he only knows what his love is. Evil people are not prepared to be shown this, and if they were shown it, they would refuse to accept it. But people who are in a heavenly love are able to be taught. They are prepared to see the evil tendencies into which they were born. They see all this on the basis of what is true, because truth does in fact show up what is evil.

On the basis, then, of a knowledge of correspondences, it is quite possible to know how the delights of a person's life are changed after death into things that correspond to them. A few illustrations of this are given.

People who have found their delight in evil loves and false ideas run away from heaven's sight. They scurry off into caves and openings in rocks and hide there. These caves and openings correspond to false ideas and evil desires, and these people find them delightful to live in whereas they would find living in the open very unpleasant. Secretive people enjoy whispering into each other's ears in the corners of rooms that are so dark that they cannot see each other. As for people who loved to collect information in order to appear clever, they love sandy places, preferring these to fields and gardens. This is because of the correspondence of such places. People who delight in religious teaching and doctrine but who do not apply them to life choose rocky places for themselves and enjoy living among piles of boulders. These, and others, are the corresponding delights that evil people come into when they enter the spiritual world after death.

In contrast, the delights of people who lived in heavenly kinds of love in the world are changed into corresponding things in heaven. Such people live in places such as lofty settings where, in front of their eyes, there are fields and crops and vineyards in a climate of springtime. Others live in houses that seem to be made of precious stones, or in gardens that are beautifully laid out, or in places where everything seems to laugh and frolic, or in transparent or wide-open places, and so on. These are only a few of the correspondences of the delights of people whose loves are heavenly.

From this it can be seen that every person's delights changed after death into things that correspond to them, with the same love enduring to eternity. This is true of marriage love, love of fairness, honesty, goodness, truth, love of knowledge and perception, love of understanding and wisdom, and so on. The things that flow from these are like brooks from a spring of water.

THE FIRST STATE OF A PERSON AFTER DEATH

There are three states that a person passes through after his death before he finally enters heaven or hell. The first state is more concerned with his outward life, the second involves his inner life, and the third is one of preparation. The person passes through these three while he is in the world of spirits. Yet there are also some people who do not pass through these three states but who enter heaven or hell almost immediately after they die. Those who immediately enter heaven are people who have been regenerated and made ready for heaven while they were in the world. Such people only need to be free of their natural impurities along with their bodies before they are taken into heaven by angels. I have seen some taken up one hour after death.

On the other hand, there are the people who appeared to be good but who were completely wicked inside. They are taken immediately into hell. I have seen people taken into hell immediately after they died — one of the most deceitful went head first. But these sorts of people are relatively few compared to the vast numbers who are kept in the world of spirits and there prepared.

The first state after death is very similar to that of life in this world. A person has much the same outward appearance to others, and much the same behaviour too. In this state, a person may be quite unaware that he is no longer in the world, unless he has understood what he was told by angels when he was awakened, that now he is a spirit. In this state too, a person is recognised by his friends and acquaintances from this world. Whenever a person in the other life thinks about someone else there, he holds the face of that person in his thought, along with many other associations, and when he does this, the other person becomes present as though he has been called or summoned.

In this first state, everyone may meet and stay together for as short or long a time as they wish to be together. If there is nothing really to keep them together, they will soon separate, often as friends taking leave of each other. But if there was conflict, this breaks out into the open and people may even fight each other. Once people have got over the surprise of having died and of now being in a body as they were in the world, they become curious to know more about what heaven and hell are like and where they are. So they are taught and taken around and led into their own thoughts about life after death. Most people are eager to know if they will get to heaven, and most believe they will because they were good people in the world. But the majority of them have no idea of deeper things or of more inward levels of life. These people are examined by good spirits to see what their qualities of life really are and certain things begin to show themselves. The evil people listen intently to everything that is said about outward things but pay almost no attention to what is said about deeper things. They hear but show no response. Also, they repeatedly head for certain areas and when left to themselves go along paths that lead to these. The quality of their lives can be detected from the areas they head for and the paths they go along.

Some people stay in this first state for a few days, some for a few months, and others a year. It rarely lasts more than a year for anyone. The length of time depends on the concord between their outer life and their inner life. And it is because each person is eventually going to become the image of his own love that the most outward levels of life must first be uncovered and put into order, to be a plane that corresponds to some inward things.

THE SECOND STATE OF A PERSON AFTER DEATH

This is called the state of interior things because now the person is let into what is in his mind, or his will and his thinking, while more outward things that were operating in the first state go to sleep. This second state is similar to the way that the person used to be in the world when he was by himself, on his own with no-one else around. He slips quite unconsciously into this state when — as he did in the world — he gives rein to the thoughts he is having that prompt what he says and becomes involved in these. As a result, when the person is in this state, he is immersed in his own self and his very own life and reveals his true nature. Now the person is beginning to think from what he really loves, scarcely seeming to think but only to will and intend. It is almost the same when he speaks, except that he talks with a kind of fear that the thoughts of his intentions might come out naked.

Everyone passes through this second state because it is the actual state of the spirit. The first state is how the person was in his spirit when he was with other people, which is not his true state.

It now becomes obvious and clear what kind of person this was while he was in the world, for at this point he behaves on the basis of what actually belongs to him and is part of him. If he was in genuine good in the world, he now acts rationally and wisely — more wisely in fact because he has been freed from physical ties and so from things which darken and tend to cloud things over. On the other hand, if he was in evil while he was in the world, he now begins to act crazily and madly — more insanely because he is now free and under no restraints.

People who have lived according to their conscience seem to themselves to wake up from a sleep when they are in this second state. For now they are thinking from the light of heaven and so from a deeper kind of wisdom than before. Once awake, they are influenced by the way in which heavenly perceptions begin to open their minds. They feel a great delight and a new sense of inner blessedness which comes from their association with angels. It is at this point that such spirits are able to recognise the Lord and to worship him through their own lives. They can see how this worship is done in complete freedom because this sense of freedom lies in their deepest affections. External worship no longer plays an important part in their lives because true worship, from within, has taken its place.

Opposed to this is the lot of those who lived in the world in complete evil, with no conscience at all and who therefore denied everything divine. Once people like this come into their inner level of life in the second state, they seem like foolish people — breaking out into violence, hatred, revenge and contempt, some being so vicious that it is almost impossible to believe that anything like them could exist inside any person. They are, in fact, in a state where they are completely free to act according to what they want to do, because they have left any external controls and restraints that would have held them in check in the world.

Since they are like this, they are sometimes reminded of what they were like in the first state. Some of them then become ashamed of themselves; some feel no shame at all, and some get angry because they are not allowed to stay as they used to be in the first state. These are shown what they would become if they were allowed this, how they would utterly destroy themselves because in time their outward life of secrecy and deceit would burn in the same way as their inner life and this would eventually consume them.

In this second state, the person visibly becomes just what he had been within himself while he was in the world, what he then did and said in secret now being openly seen. Since outside factors are not controlling at this point, spirits speak openly about such things and try to do them without any fear for their reputation as they would have once done in the world. They are also brought into many of their evils while they are in this state so that they can appear to angels and good spirits as they really are.

While evil spirits are in this second state, rushing into every sort of evil, it is usual for them to be often punished and severely so, too. There are many different kinds of punishments in the world of spirits and no distinction is made whether, in the world, one was a king or a slave. Every evil brings its own kind of punishment because the action and its consequence cannot be separated. So the person who is in some evil or other is also involved in its punishment. Yet even so, it is true to say that no-one suffers on account of the evils he did while he was in the world, but only on account of the evils that he now does; although it comes down to the same thing whether you say he suffers punishment on account of the evil things he did in the world or because of the evil things he is doing in the other life, because everyone returns after death into his own kind of life and so into the same evils. For the person is just the same as during his life in the body.

This punishment happens because it is the only means of controlling evil in this state. Encouragement no longer works, neither do teaching or fear of the law or of losing one's reputation, because outward behaviour now stems from the person's actual nature and this cannot be controlled or broken except by means of severe punishments.

Good spirits, on the other hand, are not punished at all, even if they did evil things in the world, because their evils do not come back to them after death. Their evils were of a very different sort. They did not come from a deliberate opposition to what is true; they were not done on purpose, nor from any other evil intention than that which they got from their parents by heredity.

Every person comes to the community in which his spirit was while he was in the world. His spirit is guided there little by little and eventually he reaches it and enters in. When an evil spirit is caught up in his inner state of life he is gradually turned towards his own community. Eventually he is turned straight towards it before this second state has come to an end, and when it is ended, the evil spirit hurls himself into the hell where there are those like himself. To see it, this hurling looks like falling headlong, head down and feet up, and it looks like this because the person is then in an inverted order, having loved the things of hell and rejected the things of heaven.

During this second state also, evil and good spirits are separated from each other. During the first state they were together, because so long as spirits are involved in outward things, it is the same as it was in the world, with the evil together with the good, and vice versa. This separation happens in many ways. Broadly speaking it happens by taking the evil spirits around to those communities that they were in touch with through their good thoughts and affections while they were in the first state. In this way, they are taken to those communities who were persuaded by their outward appearance that they were not evil. Now they are exposed as they really are to these spirits who, on seeing them, turn away, and as they turn away, the evil spirits also turn their faces from the good communities towards where the hellish community is that will be their destination.

THE THIRD STATE OF A PERSON AFTER DEATH

The third state can be said to be one of instruction and this state is only for people who are going to enter heaven and become angels, and not for those who will enter hell, for they cannot be taught. For those who will enter hell, the second state is also their third state which ends with their complete turning to their love and so towards the hellish community that they will enter.

Good people, however, are brought into a third state which is one of preparation for heaven by means of instruction. No-one can be prepared for heaven except by means of insights as to what is good and true, which involves instruction. It is possible, of course, to know about fairness and honesty in worldly dealings during life in the world because there are laws which teach what is right and wrong. But what is true and what is good on the spiritual level cannot be learned from the world but only from heaven. Even though people may know things from the Bible and from church teachings, yet these cannot enter a person's inner life unless he is in heaven. And a person is in heaven when he recognises what is divine and does what is fair and honest because of this. But no-one can be like this without first being taught, for example, that there is a God, that there is a heaven and a hell, that there is a life after death, that God is to be loved above all else, and that other people are to be loved as one loves oneself, and also that what is in the Bible is to be believed because it is the divine Word. Until a person sees these to be true, he cannot think spiritually, nor intend to do them, but when he does intend them, then heaven flows into his life, that is, the Lord flows into the person's life through heaven. Hence the need then for instruction. What a person only saw before to be morally honest and fair can now become the basis of his spiritual life.

Instruction, in this third state, is given by various angelic communities, in particular by those who are from the northern and southern regions of heaven because they are more concerned with things of intelligence and wisdom. There are places of instruction to which the Lord brings the good spirits who are to be taught, after their second state in the world of spirits has been completed. These places are arranged and laid out according to the types of heavenly good qualities that are to be taught. In this way everyone may be instructed in a manner which suits his own perception and character.

People are taught in a great number of different ways because they come from all sorts of different backgrounds and circumstances of life. Suitable teachers are found for all, and all teaching is done on the basis of doctrine which is drawn from the Word — not from the Word apart from doctrine.

Everyone is taught in the way that they can understand

according to their particular religion and the good teachings of their particular religion on which they based their life in the world. And teaching in the heavens differs from worldly teaching in this — in that the insights are not committed to memory but to life. They receive and take in everything that agrees with their own lives. Since this is their nature they are continually inspired by a love of what is true for the sake of usefulness in life, and the Lord provides that everyone loves the uses that fit his own nature, this love intensifying by the person's hope of becoming an angel.

When instruction is complete and the spirits are prepared for heaven, they are dressed in angelic clothes, mostly in white, like linen. Dressed in this way, they are then brought to a path that leads to heaven and they are given over to angel guardians there. Then they are received and welcomed into heavenly communities and into many kinds of happiness.

Each angel is led by the Lord to his own community. There are different paths by which this is done. No angel knows the paths by which the spirits are led, only the Lord does. As the angelic spirits reach their own community, their deepest levels of life become opened up and, because this is in complete harmony with that community, they are immediately recognised and welcomed with great joy.

NO-ONE ENTERS HEAVEN
AS A RESULT OF DIRECT MERCY

Because many people do not know what heaven is, or how it is attained, nor about the life of heaven within a person, a large number of them believe that admission into heaven is simply a matter of the Lord's mercy given to

113

people who have faith, and for whom the Lord intercedes. They imagine that one can be saved by grace out of divine goodwill. Some people even think that this also applies to those who are in hell.

Such people, however, know nothing at all about what a person really is. They do not know that a person's quality is just as his life is, and that his life is such as his love is, nor that his physical form is only an outward form through which his inward life can express itself through actions. They do not know that the body does not live from itself but from its spirit and that a person's spirit is what he loves. As long as people remain ignorant of these things, they will keep believing that salvation is nothing but the Lord's goodwill which is called mercy and grace.

It needs to be seen exactly what this divine mercy is. Divine mercy is pure mercy towards the whole of the human race and it never withdraws from a single person. So, everyone who can be saved is saved. Yet the only way anyone can be saved is by divine means which have been revealed by the Lord. These teach how a person is to live in order to be saved. By means of them, the Lord leads the person towards heaven and is able to give heavenly life. The Lord does this for everyone, but he cannot give heavenly life unless the person himself refrains from evil, because evil is what obstructs this. So far as a person refrains from evil, the Lord leads him, through his divine means, and from pure mercy, from his earliest infancy to the end of his life in the world and on into eternity. All this shows that the Lord's mercy is pure mercy but not direct mercy — that is, it is not one that would save every person from goodwill, no matter how they themselves had lived. The Lord never does anything which is contrary to his own order, or design, because he himself is the order and the design. From all this it can be seen that there is indeed no way to change anyone's life after death — an evil life can in no way be changed into a good life, or a hellish life into an angelic one. For each individual spirit is from head to toe such as his love is and such as his life is, and to change this into its opposite would mean the total destruction of his spirit.

IT IS NOT SO DIFFICULT AS PEOPLE THINK IT IS TO LIVE THE KIND OF LIFE THAT LEADS TO HEAVEN

People often have the mistaken idea that it is very hard to live the kind of life that leads to heaven. They have heard that one needs to renounce the world, give up every pleasure to do with the body, and live spiritually. They imagine that this means that the world, with all its riches and honour, must be shunned, that one must go around meditating on God, on salvation and eternal life, in continual prayer and Bible reading, and so on. But this simply is not the case. In fact, people who give up the world like this end up making life miserable for themselves, a life that cannot receive heavenly joy at all since every person's life stays with him when he dies.

If a person is to receive the life of heaven he has to live in the world and be involved in its affairs and business. For then, through a moral and public life he can receive a spiritual life. There is no other way that spiritual life can be formed in a person or that his spirit can be prepared for heaven. This is because to live an inner kind of life without at the same time living an outward life is just like living in a house which doesn't have any foundations, a house which gradually sinks, or becomes cracked, or which totters until it falls down. Spiritual living is not removed from natural living, nor from living in the world, but rather they are bound together, just as the soul is with the body.

Life is threefold: it is spiritual, it is moral and it is public. There are people who live a public life who do not lead a moral or spiritual one; there are people who live a moral life but still not a spiritual one. And there are people who live all three — public, moral and spiritual — and these are the ones who are leading the heavenly life.

Moral and public life are the active side of spiritual life. If what is spiritual is separated from them, it is nothing but thinking and talking, a way of life that has no real basis to it.

Everyone can live a moral and public life. Everyone is familiar with what it is from his life in the world. Everyone, good or bad, leads it as well, for who does not want to be called honest and fair? A spiritual person needs to live in the same way, which he can do just as easily as a natural person, with the difference that he believes in the divine and behaves honestly and fairly not just because it is in keeping with public and moral laws but because it is a matter of divine law. When someone is like this, he is led by the Lord without realising it. Then what he does as part of his public and moral life is done from a spiritual source as well. The ten commandments contain all the laws of spiritual life, public life and moral life. These are given by the Lord for the whole of humanity. The first three of the commandments are to do with spiritual life, the next four with public life, and the last three with moral life.

All this is said to show that a life which leads to heaven cannot be achieved by separation from the world. A pious life without loving action is unable to lead to heaven. Rather, what does lead to heaven is a life of love in useful activity — behaving fairly and honestly in every task, every transaction, every work, and this from an interior or heavenly motive which is present when a person acts justly because it is in keeping with divine laws.

This life is not hard; rather, the life of piety separate from a life of loving activity is harder to live and this leads a person away from heaven just as surely as some believe that it leads to heaven.

LIFE IN HELL

THE LORD CONTROLS THE HELLS

It was shown earlier, in dealing with heaven, that the Lord is the God of heaven and that the whole organisation of heaven is from him. Accepting that the relationship between heaven and hell is that of two opposite forces that work against each other, from which a perfect balance results to keep everything in existence, it follows that he who controls one must control the other too. For unless the Lord set limits on the outbursts from hell and checked its mad desires, this equilibrium would be destroyed and with it everything else.

It is a well-known fact that when two opposing forces work against each other to the same extent neither of them has any power because there is an equal force on each side. The balance can then be determined by a third party just as easily as if there were no opposition, and the action of the third party is in complete control.

There is this kind of equilibrium between heaven and hell. Not that it is the kind you would expect to find between two strong men in a fight. Rather, it is a spiritual balance of what is false against what is true and of what is evil against what is good. It is this balance that enables a person to be free in his thinking and in what he intends, for whatever a person thinks or wishes has to do with either evil and falsity or what is good and true. So when someone is in this balance he is free to let in the one or the other.

Every person is held in this balance by the Lord because he rules over both heaven and hell and therefore controls their influences. The influence of evil is like a never-ending effort to destroy what is good, along with an anger and outrage at not being able to do so. The influence of good is to curb and restrain hell's ragings and thereby is the balance created.

Power in the spiritual world is only with what is good and true because these come from the Divine and all power belongs to the Divine. Evil and falsity have no real power because in them there is nothing of what is good or true at all. So all power is in heaven and none in hell.

People who are in the world of spirits are in this same balance or equilibrium because the world of spirits is midway between heaven and hell. As a result, all people in the world are held in the same balance too, because they are governed by the Lord through spirits who are in the world of spirits.

This balance would not exist at all if the Lord did not have control over both heaven and hell and regulate both sides. Were he not to do this, then evil would increase to the extent that it would influence and mislead simple good people and the balance of freedom would be destroyed.

Hell is made up of different communities in the way that heaven is and there are the same number of communities in each since each community in heaven has its opposite community in hell. Nothing exists without its opposite, and the nature of something can be known by looking at what is opposite to it. So, for the sake of equilibrium, the Lord provides that each community of heaven has its counterpart in a community of hell.

In addition to this, it is worth noting that each community in hell is a hell in miniature, just as heavenly communities are also heavens in miniature. And there are three hells just as there are three heavens. The lowest hell is opposite to the inmost or highest heaven, the middle hell to the middle or second heaven, and the highest — or mildest — hell to the outermost or first heaven.

HOW THE LORD CONTROLS THE HELLS

The hells are controlled by the Lord's own influence which proceeds through the heavens and the communities there and which curbs evil at its source. Specifically, the control is done through angels who are given the ability to inspect the hells and to control the outbursts there. From time to time, angels are sent into hell where they calm things down by their presence.

Generally speaking though, people in hell are controlled simply by their own fears.

Some are controlled by fears they had while they were in the world, although these may lessen in time. So the fear of being punished takes over which deters many of them from doing evil, for punishment itself is a deterrent to evil people. For the most part, the more vicious people in hell are given power over the others. They are devious and scheming and they are able to hold everyone in subjection and slavery to them by punishments and terror. Yet these so-called rulers are afraid to go beyond the limits that have been set for them. The fear of punishment is the only way of controlling the ferocity and violence of people in hell. There is no other way.

People in the world have believed that there is one overall Devil who rules over the hells; more, that he was created as an angel of light but that, after causing a rebellion, he was cast into hell with his crew. People have believed this because the Devil and Satan, and Lucifer, are mentioned in the Bible and they have taken these literally. Yet 'Devil' and 'Satan' simply mean hell in its various degrees of evil, while 'Lucifer' means the people in hell who reach out into the heavens and try to influence those there. There is no one devil to whom those in hell are subject. Everyone in hell is from the human race and every one of them is a devil from his complete opposition to the Divine that made him human while he was in the world.

IT IS NOT THE LORD WHO CASTS PEOPLE INTO HELL BUT THE PERSON HIMSELF WHO DOES SO

Some people have the idea that God turns his face away from a person, that he rejects him and casts him away from himself into hell, and is angry with him because of his evils. Some people even believe that God punishes a person and does evil to him. They support these ideas with literal statements from the Bible, not realising that the spiritual meaning of the Bible is completely different, or that the true teaching of the church is that God never turns his face away from any person, never casts him away, and never casts anyone into hell or becomes angry like this.

Any enlightened person can see, when he reads the Bible, that God is goodness itself, love itself, mercy itself, and that he is therefore unable to do evil to anyone. Love cannot cast a person from itself because this goes against the very nature of love, and therefore against the divine nature itself. If people think with enlightened minds, they will see that God deals with people from goodness, love, and mercy, wanting what is good for them, loving them, and having mercy on them. They see that, since good and evil are opposites, nothing but what is good can come out of heaven or flow in from the Lord who, therefore, is continually leading each person away from evil and towards what is good. And as there is the balance between heaven and hell, were the Lord to turn away and a person be left only to what is evil, he would no longer be a person.

From this we can see that the Lord flows into all people with what is good — into an evil person just as much as into a good person. But with a difference; he continually leads an evil person away from what is evil but he continually leads a good person towards what is good. The difference is in the person, not in the Lord. It is clear then that a person does what is evil because of hell and does what is good because of the Lord. But since the person believes that whatever he does he does on his own, when he does something evil it sticks to him as though it were his own. This is why the person, and never the Lord, is responsible for his own evil. Therefore it is he who leads himself to hell and not the Lord. Far from leading any person to hell, the Lord frees people from hell so far as the person does not want to do his own evil or be in it.

A person's intention and love stay with him after death so that he who loves evil in the world will love the same evil in the other life and will not let himself be led away from it. So an evil person is tied to hell and, so far as his spirit is concerned, is already there, and after death wants nothing so much as to be where his own evil is. Consequently after death the person himself, and not the Lord, casts himself into hell.

What happens after death can be briefly described. When a person enters the world of spirits he is welcomed by angels who help in every way they can, talking about the Lord and life in heaven. But if the person had known about these in the world and there had denied them or sneered at them, then he soon longs to get away. When the angels note this, they leave him. Eventually he joins up with people just like himself, and turns away from the Lord to face the hell he had been linked with while he was in the world. In spite of every possible assistance from heaven, such a spirit will follow his own evil and eventually — and freely — cast himself into his own hell.

THOSE IN HELL ARE IN WHAT IS EVIL AND FALSE AS A RESULT OF THEIR OWN SELF-LOVE AND LOVE OF THE WORLD

Everyone in hell is caught up in evil and false things only; no-one is there who is in both evil and true things at the same time. Evil people can be very familiar with spiritual ideas while they are in the world, hearing them, learning them, reading about them and talking about them. Some of them even dupe other people into believing that they are heartfelt Christians by their talk and their apparent good behaviour.

But all such people are only evil at heart, and once their outward life is stripped away from them they come into their true colours. What was apparently good or true in them was only in their memory, like information, which they were able to take out at will and use for their own

124

ends. When such people are let into their true natures, they cannot say anything true any more, but only what is false, because they speak from evil. It is impossible to speak the truth on the basis of what is evil, only false ideas will come out.

When a person is like this after death, his body and his face correspond to what lies within him. People can, at this time, tell exactly what he is like by looking at him; not just from his face but from his whole body and his speech and the way he behaves. When spirits in hell are examined in any light of heaven, they look just like their evil qualities. Each one is a replica of his evil. They become visible forms of contempt, menace, hatred, revenge, fury and cruelty. And yet, when someone else praises them or flatters them for some reason, their faces are more restrained and something like a happy look from the pleasure they feel appears on them.

The appearance of these evil spirits is frightful to see. Some have swollen faces, or ones that are full of open sores. Many have no actual face but only something hairy or bony. With some the teeth stand right out. Their bodies are grotesque. Yet it has to be understood that while hellish spirits look like this in heaven's light, they look like ordinary people to each other. This is arranged for by the Lord so that their own state may not be for them the way it looks to angels.

All of these spirits are embodiments of either self-love or love of the world.

These two loves reign supreme in hell and make hell. They are in complete opposition to the two heavenly loves which are love to the Lord and the neighbour. Many people cannot see why these two loves — self-love and love of the world — are so diabolical. They say that pride, when it is visible, is something far worse. And they add that everyone tends to do things for the sake of praise and self-glory. They do not realise that self-love is the controlling love in hell and that it makes hell in a person.

So self-love needs to be described in more detail, because it is the fountain of all other evil loves. Self-love is to wish well to oneself only and not to anyone else, unless it benefits oneself. It involves doing good to others only for the purpose of glory and honour. Unless the person sees these benefits in what he is doing for others, he asks himself, "What shall I get from this?" and so he does not do it. His happiness is purely the happiness of self-love and since this delight from love makes the person's life, his life becomes a life of self. Such a person can love people who in some way belong to him, like his wife and children, whom he calls his own. Included in these are all the people who praise him or obey him.

By contrast, heavenly love is loving what is useful for its own sake and this is actually loving God and the neighbour. But if a person loves what is useful only for his own sake, he loves these things as slaves who work for him. He wants everything and everyone to work for him and not the other way round. Someone who is wrapped up in his own self-interest focuses on himself in any good that he does. This happens because he looks for himself in the doing and not out from himself to the good he could do.

Self-love turns people, as it were, upside down and they appear in the spiritual world to be falling towards hell with their feet pointing towards heaven. It is due to this that people who freely enter hell seem to fall headfirst in that direction.

Love of the world is not so opposed to heavenly love as self-love is because its particular evils are less harmful ones. Love of the world is the desire to get for oneself the wealth of others, and this by any means possible. It is to set one's heart on riches and to let the world lead one away from any spiritual love. It can take many forms. There is the love of wealth for the sake of personal advancement; there is the love of status as the means to getting more wealth; there is the love of wealth as a means towards having worldly pleasures; there is the love of wealth for its own sake, such as avaricious people have. The list is endless.

Wealth indeed may be of great use and the purpose behind it is its use. The end in view is what gives love its own quality, for the two are exactly the same. Everything else merely serves it as means.

HELL-FIRE AND GNASHING OF TEETH

Most people do not know what else could be meant by hell-fire and gnashing of teeth when they are mentioned in the Bible than a literal description of these things in hell. Some think that the fire is an actual one, or perhaps a kind of torment, like pangs of conscience. Some see hell-fire as a phrase that is used to terrify wicked people. Some people think that the gnashing of teeth actually happens or that it stands for the kind of fear there is when you hear teeth chatter like this. Yet both of them must be understood spiritually, for what is spiritual can only be expressed to people through natural images which people can understand. Hell-fire and gnashing of teeth are certainly a part of the lives of evil peoples' spirits after death or, to put it another way, they will undergo these things in the spiritual world. Hence they need to be properly understood. First, about hell-fire itself. There are two sources of heat; one from the sun of heaven which is the Lord himself and the other from the sun of this world. Heat which comes from the Lord as the spiritual sun is a spiritual heat which is love. The heat we feel from the world's sun is purely natural and it brings about growth in nature. This growth reflects the spiritual flow of heavenly heat, or love, into peoples' spirits which activates their whole being. A natural phenomenon does not happen or exist unless it is the result — or the correspondence — of a spiritual cause. Even the things in nature have their ability to germinate and grow from the influence of the spiritual world.

For people, spiritual heat is the heat of their life because it is essentially love. This heat is what is meant in the Bible by 'fire', heavenly fire being love to the Lord and the neighbour and hellish fire being self-love and love of the world. Hellish fire or love is actually from the same source as heavenly fire — from the sun of heaven, or the Lord. It is made hellish by the people who receive it and distort it. For all the flowing-in from the spiritual world varies depending on how it is received or on the forms into which it flows. This is exactly the same as with the warmth and light that come from the world's sun. When it is received by trees and plants it makes them grow and give off scents. But when it is received by dead or dirty matter it brings about decay and rotten smells. When love flows into the lives of good people, spirits and angels, it makes their good bear fruit. But with evil people it has the opposite effect and it is stifled or corrupted.

Since hell-fire, then, is self-love and love of the world, it shows the cravings that belong to these loves. It also shows the pleasures of them too. This is why, in the spiritual world, when hell opens, fire and smoke can actually be seen coming from them. And when they are closed up, the fire is seen to be smouldering. This is from correspondence.

Yet the people in hell are not in fire as such; the fire is an appearance. They are not conscious of any burning, only of the same kind of heat that they felt while they were in the world.

This hell-fire also means the kind of torment that there is in hell, a torment which comes from a craving to injure other people and the anger that goes with it. It may be wondered, of course, why evil spirits cast themselves willingly into hell, as has been said, if there are such torments there. Every hell breathes out its own sphere — its own craving — which comes from those who are there. When this is sensed by someone who has the same craving, he is filled with delight, turns toward it and craves to get to it. At this point, however, he does not actually realise the kind of torment that there is there, but even though he did he would still crave. When he is there in his hell he is welcomed warmly at first and he believes that he is among friends. However, this lasts only for a few hours. All this time he is being closely watched to see how clever he is and how strong he is. Once this is known, they attack him in different ways, gradually increasing the severity and the violence. They do this by leading him further and further into hell, for the deeper one goes, the more vicious the spirits are. After attacking him like this, they take it out on him by punishing him until he is reduced to slavery. Yet rebellions are always springing up there, because everyone wants to be the most important of all and is burning with hatred against all the others, and there are new uprisings all the time. One situation gives way to another. Enslaved members are freed to give their help to new leaders in order to conquer others. Then those who refuse to obey are tormented again, and this goes on and on. These torments of hell are called hell-fire.

Gnashing of teeth, on the other hand, is the continual conflict and clash of false ideas with each other, in people who are in such things and who have contempt for others, animosity, mockery, derision and blasphemy. These evils burst out into wounding, cutting, clawing and scratching because everyone is fighting for all he is worth for his own false ideas and calling them true. These conflicts are heard outside the hells like gnashing teeth and they are turned into gnashing teeth whenever what is true flows in from heaven.

The people who live in these hells are those who only believed in nature and who denied the Lord. They are incapable of receiving any light from heaven and most of them will believe nothing but what their eyes can see and their hands can touch. This is why their arguments sound like gnashing teeth, for in the spiritual world all false ideas give a grating sound, and teeth themselves correspond to the lowest things of nature and the outermost things in people.

THE MALICE AND CUNNING OF HELLISH SPIRITS

Anyone who thinks deeply about things and understands to some extent how his own mind works, can see how far spirits surpass people in their abilities. A person can turn over in his mind more things in a minute, and sort them out and draw conclusions from them, than he could speak about or put down in writing in half an hour. How much more able, then, he becomes when he is a spirit! For it is the spirit that thinks and the body that expresses the thoughts in speech or writing. As a result, the person who becomes an angel after death has intelligence and wisdom that is indescribable in comparison to that which he had in the world, for there his spirit was bound by his body so that anything he thought about flowed into relatively crude and obscure vessels.

But when his spirit is released from the body and he has come into his own life, it is completely different. His condition now vastly surpasses what it was before. This is why angels have indescribable thoughts, the kind of thoughts that can never enter a person's mind. And yet every angel was born as a human being and during his life seemed to himself to be no wiser than any other person.

The malice and cunning of hellish spirits is just as great as the wisdom and intelligence of angels. The situation is the same, since after a person's death, his spirit becomes absorbed completely in his own good or his own evil. A consistency comes into being which increases the thinking of each.

It was different, though, while the person was in the world, for there the evil part of the person's spirit was under restraints and so could not break out into the open. It was more than likely covered over by an outward appearance of good behaviour and affections, so much so that even the person himself scarcely knew what malice and cunning existed in his spirit, nor that he was such a devil as he was to become after death, when his spirit came fully into its own nature.

Such malice then shows itself as is beyond all belief. Thousands of evils burst out from evil itself. Hardly one in a thousand can be described. They are so malignant that, if the Lord were not to protect every person, they would never escape hell. For spirits from hell are with each person, just as angels from heaven are. The Lord cannot protect a person unless he recognises the Divine and lives a life that is based on faith and loving actions. If this is not the case, the person turns away from the Lord toward hellish spirits, taking into himself the same kinds of malice. Yet even so, he is continually being led away from his own evil by the Lord and, if the Lord cannot lead him by these inner restraints of conscience, then he leads him by means of outward restraints such as fear of the law and of punishment.

Yet, even though a person may be led away, he cannot be led into anything spiritual because, if he were, he would create devious and deceitful ways of imitating and pretending things that are honest and fair, all of which simply increases the evil of his spirit and shapes it, making him as evil as he is in his own nature.

The worst of all are those whose evil stems from self-love. Their deceit permeates so thoroughly that they are full of poison which destroys their whole life. These spirits are called 'genii' and they are towards the back of the hells. Those who were evil as a result of their love of the world are towards the front part of the hells and they are called 'spirits'. They are not so malignant and their hells are milder.

Genii do not work on a person's thoughts but into his affections. They watch and smell them out. When they detect good affections, they turn them into evil ones by twisting and leading them, using the person's own delights. They do this so secretly that the person does not know anything about it. They manage this by taking great care that nothing of this comes into the person's thinking, for they would be exposed. These genii are people who entrap peoples' minds by using their pleasures and desires to lead and sway them.

They are held back by the Lord from any person in whom there is any hope of change. They are the kind of beings who not only have the ability to destroy peoples' consciences, but also to stir up hereditary things within them, things which otherwise would have stayed hidden. So, to prevent a person being led into these, the Lord provides that these hells are completely closed off. When a person who is like them comes into the other life, he is instantly cast into their hell.

The cunning of hellish spirits is so varied that it would take many books to describe them. They are almost unknown in the world. One sort is to do with the abuse of correspondences; another with the misuse of the lower things of divine order; a third, with different kinds of communication and flow of thoughts by using conversions, searchings, and by using other spirits apart from themselves, and others sent out by themselves; a fourth, with fantasies; a fifth, with spirit-projection to create a presence where there is not one; a sixth, which involves impersonation, persuasion and lies.

Hellish spirits torment each other by using all these skills, and an evil spirit comes into them after death if they are part of his own evil at this point.

The reason that torments in the hells are tolerated by the

Lord is that this is the only way that evil can be controlled and held in check. The only means of keeping the hellish crew under control is by using the fear of punishment; no other way exists. For without the fear of punishment and torment, evil would burst out into raging violence, and everything would go to pieces, just as happens to kingdoms in the world where there is no law and where there are no punishments.

THE APPEARANCE, LOCATION, AND NUMBER OF THE HELLS

In the spiritual world, one can see the same sort of things that exist in the natural world. They are so much alike that outwardly there is no difference. One can see plains, mountains, hills and rocks, with valleys between them, and lakes and rivers along with many other things that can be seen in the world. Even so, all of these things come from a spiritual origin and so they are visible to spirits and angels but not to people. As a result, a person can never see with his own eyes the things that are in the spiritual world unless he is allowed to be in the spirit, or after death when he becomes a spirit. In the same way, a spirit or angel is not able to see anything in the natural world unless he is with a person who is allowed to speak with him. As there is this similarity between the spiritual world and the natural world, after death the person hardly notices that he is not in the world that he has just left behind. This is why death is simply called a crossing over from one world into another like it.

The heavens are in the more elevated regions of the spiritual world, the world of spirits is lower, and the hells are below both of them. Heaven itself is not visible to spirits in the world of spirits except when their inner sight is opened; although sometimes they are visible as mists or bright clouds. This is because angels have a higher wisdom than others and so they are above the sight of people who are in the world of spirits.

But spirits who are in the plains and valleys can see each other. When, though, they are sorted out into their true natures, the evil spirits can no longer see the good spirits. The good spirits can still see the evil ones, but turn themselves away from them, and when spirits turn away they become invisible. The hells are not visible because they are closed up. Only the entrances to them can be seen, when they open to let people in who are like those who are there. The entrances to hell only open from the world of spirits — none of them open from heaven.

The hells are everywhere — under mountains, hills and rocks; under the plains and valleys. Every one of them is dark and gloomy and yet the hellish spirits who are there are in the kind of light that burning torches give. Their eyes are adapted to receive this light. They regard the light of heaven as profound darkness, and if they were to leave their caves they would be unable to see at all.

All the openings to hell are hidden and out of sight except when evil spirits are going in from the world of spirits. Yet, when it pleases the Lord, a spirit or angel who is above the hells can, with his sight, penetrate them to the very depths and see what they are like, as if there were no coverings. Some hells look like caverns, others look like lairs and dens, some are like the passages in mines with caves at the bottom. In certain hells one can see piles of rubble as if after a great fire, where hellish spirits live and hide. In the milder hells are seen tumbledown huts crowded together. Inside the hovels are hellish spirits and there is non-stop brawling, beating, clawing, robberies and quarrels. In some of the hells there are nothing but brothels, in others dark forest, where spirits roam about like wild animals and where there are underground tunnels into which spirits flee when pursued by others. There are also deserts where spirits who have suffered every possible punishment are driven. And there are others.

Only the Lord knows the exact location of the hells, although in general their position can be understood from the regions that they are in. The hells are divided into regions just as the heavens are and the divisions are based on the kinds of loves there are. Every spiritual region is positioned in relation to the Lord as the sun who is in the east. Since the hells are opposite to the heavens, their regions start from the west and get worse and worse as they get farther from the east. It is not really possible to know how the hells are arranged. All we can know is that the most dreadul of them are on the side towards the north and the less dreadful are towards the south. On the eastern side are the milder hells, such as those who were proud but not full of intense hatred.

As for the number of hells, it is sufficient to say that there are as many hells as there are heavenly communities because each heavenly community has its corresponding opposite community in hell. The number of hells is beyond counting — there are even hells that are under hells.

People will appreciate none of this if they only have a simplistic idea of such things as contempt, enmity, hatred, revenge, deceit and the like. Let them realise that every single one of these comprises so many types and each of these again so many different species that a whole book would not be enough to list them.

THE BALANCE BETWEEN HEAVEN AND HELL

The existence of a balance — or equilibrium — between heaven and hell has already been mentioned at the beginning of this section on 'Hell', but more needs to be said about it because it is such a key factor in understanding heaven and hell as a whole.

Everything has to be in a balance if anything is to result. Without a balance there is no action and reaction, for equilibrium is between two forces, one acting and the other reacting. The state of rest that comes about from an equal action and reaction is called equilibrium.

There is a balance in the natural world as a whole and also in each thing in it. The lower atmosphere, for example, reacts and resists in proportion to the action and pressing down of the higher atmosphere. There is a balance in the natural world between heat and cold, light and shade, dryness and moisture, and the middle point between them forms the balance. Everything happens by one force flowing in and the other accepting it or giving way to it. In the natural world these are called force and effort, but in the spiritual world they are called life and will, or intention. In that world, life is a living force, and will is a living effort. The balance is called freedom.

So spiritual balance, or freedom, comes into being and continues from the action of good on the one side and the reaction of evil on the other, or from the action of evil and the reaction of good. There is a balance between good

137

acting and evil reacting in good people, and between evil acting and good reacting in evil people. All this is because every part of a person's life is to do with what is good and what is evil, and the person's will is the receptacle.

There is a perpetual balance between heaven and hell. An effort to do what is evil constantly breathes up out of hell, and an effort to do what is good continually breathes down from heaven. The world of spirits is in perfect balance between the two because it is halfway between heaven and hell. It is in this balance because every person enters first into the world of spirits after death and is kept there in the same kind of state he was in while he was in the world. This would not be possible unless there was this perfect balance there. By means of this balance everyone is examined carefully to find out what he is like, since people there are just as free as they were in the world.

The reason that evil breathes from hell and good breathes from heaven is because each individual person is encompassed by a spiritual sphere which flows out from the person's affections and from his thoughts. As with each individual, so with whole communities of both heaven and hell; their combined sphere flows forth, that is, from heaven as a whole and from hell as a whole.

Good flows from heaven because everyone there is involved in what is good. Evil flows from hell because everyone there is involved in what is evil. Yet the good which flows from heaven comes from the Lord who keeps all the angels away from their own selfhood and keeps them in his own image. Whereas those who are in the hells are involved only in their own selfhood, and this in itself is nothing but evil. Since it is only evil, it is hell.

In this way, it can be seen that the balance in which angels in heaven and spirits in hell are kept is not like the balance that is found in the world of spirits. The balance for angels in heaven is a matter of the extent to which they wanted to be involved in what is good — or lived in doing good while they were in the world — and how much they turned away from what is evil. And the balance for spirits in hell is a matter of the extent to which they wanted to be involved in what is evil — or lived evilly during their lives — and how opposed they were to the good in their heart and their spirit.

If the Lord did not govern and regulate both heaven and hell, there would be no balance, and if there were no balance, there would be no heaven and hell. The balance between heaven and hell is affected by the number of people entering them, which amounts to several thousand a day. No angel can know this or do anything about it. Only the Lord can do this, because the Divine is present everywhere and sees just which way a given situation is leaning. So the Lord is constantly taking care to prevent a given hellish community from getting too strong. As one does, certain measures are taken to confine it and bring it back to the balance. Some of these measures involve the closer presence of the Lord himself; some, a closer communication of one community with others; others, the banishment of excess evil spirits to desert places or to other hells, and so on. The point is that it is the Lord alone who sees to it that there is a balance, because on this balance rests the salvation of all the people in heaven and on earth. Hell is constantly attacking heaven and trying to destroy it, while the Lord constantly protects it by keeping the people in heaven away from their own selfhood and in the good which comes from him. On the other hand, heaven in no way attacks hell, because the sphere which comes from the Lord is an unceasing effort to save everyone. Since the people in hell cannot be saved, as they were caught up in what is evil and thus opposed to the Lord, they are restrained as much as they can be, and confined so that they do not burst out against each other beyond certain limits.

PEOPLE ARE IN FREEDOM BECAUSE OF THIS BALANCE BETWEEN HEAVEN AND HELL

Spiritual balance is freedom itself because it is a balance between what is good and what is evil. The freedom which is here meant is the ability to intend either good or evil and to choose one rather than the other.

This freedom is given to each person by the Lord and it is never taken away. It is something that belongs to the Lord and not to the person, and yet it is given to each person with his life just as if it were his own, so that he may be reformed and saved; without this freedom, neither of these would be possible. Clearly, it lies within the scope of a person's freedom to think either badly or well, honestly or dishonestly, fairly or unfairly, and also to speak and act well, honestly, and fairly. Yet because of spiritual, moral and civil laws which put restraints on the outer conduct of life, this freedom is not equally true of speaking and acting badly, dishonestly, or unfairly.

It is a person's spirit — the part in him that thinks and intends — that is in this freedom. The same cannot be said for the outward part of a person which speaks and acts, unless it is in agreement with the laws just mentioned.

The reason that a person cannot be reformed without this spiritual freedom is because he is born into all sorts of

140

evils which need to be taken away if he is going to be saved. They cannot be taken away unless he sees them in himself and recognises them; identifies what they are; no longer wants to do them; and finally turns away from them. Then for the first time they are taken away. This will not happen unless the individual is as much involved in what is good as in what is evil, since it is from good that he is able to see evil, while from evil he cannot see good. The good that a person is capable of thinking is formed from what he learns in childhood, from reading the Bible and hearing it explained. He also learns what is morally good from living in the world.

A second reason for the need to be in freedom is that nothing becomes part of a person unless it happens as a result of an affection to do with his love. All manner of things may come into him but they come no further than his thinking and they do not enter his will. And what does not enter right into a person's will does not belong to him, because thought draws from the memory, while will or intention is drawn from life itself. A person's spirit is linked both to heaven and to hell in order to maintain him in freedom so that he can be reformed and saved. There are spirits from hell and angels from heaven with every single person. In this way, a person is in spiritual balance and therefore in freedom. But it should be understood that a person's link with heaven and hell is not direct, but indirect, through spirits who are in the midway world of spirits. These spirits are with the person; no-one from hell itself or heaven itself is with him. The person is linked with hell through spirits in the world of spirits, and with heaven through good spirits there.

As this is the way in which everything is arranged the world of spirits is midway between heaven and hell, and the actual balance occurs there. Spirits who are attached to people are sent out from a particular community to the person. This particular spirit is called the group's 'subject' spirit. A whole community can be in communication with another community or with an individual in this way. This is how communication works in the spiritual world; it works in the same way between a person in this world and communities in the spiritual world. Subject spirits from the world of spirits are attached to him.

Finally, a few words need to be said about peoples' notion of life after death, a notion into which people are born and which comes from the flowing in of heaven into people. There is an innate idea of life after death with every person who is linked with heaven. Its origin and source is an influence from heaven, or rather, from the Lord through heaven, by means of spirits who are attached to the person from the world of spirits. People have this notion if their freedom of thought has not been blotted out by wrong ideas about the human soul, such as that the soul is pure thought or is something merely present in the body. For in fact, the soul is nothing else than the person's life, and the spirit is the actual person. The physical body he carries around in the world is simply a servant through which the spirit is able to act in a natural world.

POSTSCRIPT

Everything that has been said in this book will seem strange to people who find no delight in spiritual things, but they will be clear to those who do find this delight. This will be particularly true for those peole who love what is true for its own sake and because it is true. In fact, anything that is loved brings its own light into the mind, especially when the truth is loved, because everything true is in the light.

APPENDIX

Swedenborg's title was *"De Caelo et eius Mirabilibus, et de Inferno, ex Auditis et Visis"*, usually translated, *"Heaven and its Wonders, and Hell, from things heard and seen"*.

He numbered each paragraph in his book, and headed each section with a title, sometimes a lengthy proposition. These are given here in full, to give some idea of the whole book, and assist reference to it.

INDEX

151

153

Seminar Books are published by
The Missionary Society of the New Church,
Swedenborg House, 20-21 Bloomsbury Way,
London WC1A 2TH.

Distributed by New Church House,
34 John Dalton Street, Manchester M2 6LE.

The writings of Emanuel Swedenborg (1688-1772)
are published by Swedenborg Society,
Swedenborg House, 20-21 Bloomsbury Way,
London WC1A 2TH.

Also by the Swedenborg Foundation
in the United States of America.
The Swedenborg Foundation
320 North Church Street
West Chester PA 19380
U.S.A.

READING LIST

The full 'Heaven and Hell' and a few other books by Swedenborg

Heaven and Hell (Swedenborg Society)
a cautious traditional translation

Heaven and Hell (Swedenborg Foundation)
translated into more idiomatic modern English
large print edition

The New Jerusalem (Swedenborg Society)
his best short general book

Divine Providence (Swedenborg Society)
how the Lord does everything possible
to lead us all to heaven, but not to force us

Books presenting ideas from Heaven and Hell in other ways

Wilson Van Dusen: *The Presence of Other Worlds* (Swedenborg Foundation 1974)

Bruce Henderson: *Window to Eternity* (Swedenborg Foundation 1987)

Brian Kingslake: *The Aqueduct Papers* (Seminar Books 1987) imaginative letters from an angel

Books presenting Swedenborg's wider thought

Brian Kingslake: *Inner Light* (J. Appleseed & Co. 1991)

Michael Stanley: *Emanuel Swedenborg: Essential Readings* (Crucible 1988)

A full catalogue of Swedenborg's writings may be obtained from The Swedenborg Society
Swedenborg House, 20-21 Bloomsbury Way, London WC1A 2TH.
Other books about him may also be obtained from the same address or from New Church House, 34 John Dalton Street, Manchester M2 6LE who will be pleased to supply American publications.